Subtle Shifts

Subtle *Shifts*

Simple Strategies for Sustainable Success

MATT CROSS

Published by Inflection Point Press
First published in 2025 in Connecticut, USA
Copyright © Matt Cross

The moral rights of the author have been asserted.

All rights reserved. No part of this publication may be used or reproduced, stored in a retrieval system, or transmitted in any form or by any means without the publisher's prior written consent.

Every effort has been made to trace (and seek permission for the use of) the original source of material used within this book. Where the attempt has been unsuccessful, the publisher would be pleased to hear from the author to rectify any omission.

All inquiries should be made to the author.

Edited by Jenny Magee
Cover design by Rafal Tomal
Designed and typeset in Australia by BookPOD

ISBN: 979-8-9929235-0-6 (hardback)
ISBN: 979-8-9929235-1-3 (paperback)
ISBN: 979-8-9929235-2-0 (e-book)

To Sadie

Contents

Preface   ix
Introduction   1

PART 1   SHIFTING ATTENTION

1. EVALUATE: Pay Attention to Your Attention   21
2. ELIMINATE: Discard Distracting Desires   37
3. ELEVATE: Focus on What Matters Most   61

PART 2   SHIFTING ASSUMPTIONS

4. CONTEMPLATE: Think About Your Thinking   89
5. COLLABORATE: Ask Others For Help   109
6. UPDATE: Embrace Empowering Assumptions   127

PART 3   SHIFTING ACTIONS

7. FORMULATE: Start with Strategy   151
8. CALIBRATE: Align your Actions   169
9. NAVIGATE: Finding the Sweet Spot   189

Conclusion   211
Before You Close This Book...   219
About the Author   220
Notes   222
Beyond the Book   231

subtle /sŭt′l/

adjective

1. So slight as to be difficult to detect or describe; elusive.
2. Difficult to understand; abstruse.
3. Able to make fine distinctions.

shift /shĭft/

intransitive verb

1. To exchange (one thing) for another of the same class.
2. To move or transfer from one place or position to another.
3. To alter (position or place).[1]

Preface

Philosophers from Aristotle to modern-day thinkers have weighed in with interpretations of the concept of change. But if you're delving into this book, you're likely not seeking a theoretical exploration. Instead, you're eager to understand how profound change is initiated, why it resonates deeply, and perhaps how you can be an agent of meaningful transformation. If that's the case, welcome. I'm thrilled, as that's precisely the territory I'm passionate about navigating.

Whether you're a manager aiming to inspire a team, an executive leading a large-scale change initiative, an entrepreneur wanting to pivot into a new venture, or an individual who wants to change something in your life, this book is for you.

Why do we struggle with change? Biology is partly to blame. When confronted with dramatic changes, the brain can perceive them as threats, triggering our natural defense mechanisms. Change is hard because we get in our own way.

In 2022, companies spent more than US$380 billion globally on professional development, and consumers ponied up US$40 billion for personal development.[2,3] The hunger for growth and change is insatiable. Change is a timeless tide, and our need to evolve is always present. But so many of us fail to embrace evolution as a strategy.

In the early 2010s, the department store JCPenney embarked on a radical overhaul under CEO Ron Johnson. Eager to modernize, Johnson swiftly introduced several sweeping changes to the business. He replaced nearly all the company's top executives, axed thousands of middle managers, eliminated employee commissions, and dramatically changed the company's pricing structure and business model.

These abrupt changes left JCPenney's employees and loyal customers feeling adrift. They had grown accustomed to and even cherished the business culture, seasonal discounts, and the thrill of a deal. As sales sharply declined, the company quickly realized the pitfalls of sidelining evolution in favor of a hasty revolution. By the time they reverted to their original strategy, the damage was done, and the company reported a net loss of just under $1 billion in 2012.[4]

Contrast Johnson's leadership with Steve Jobs, his former colleague at Apple. While many view Jobs as a trailblazer who championed radical change, closer examination reveals a subtler truth. After being exiled from Apple and returning in 1997, Jobs led Apple to transform the tech landscape.

While the world watched in awe (with Johnson possibly among them), Jobs didn't enact rapid, sweeping changes. Instead, he removed barriers to collaboration, dismantled the silos, and shifted the culture over time. With a discerning eye, he reduced Apple's sprawling product lineup to a handful of beautifully crafted devices.

Change is an evolution, not a revolution.

He spoke about the changes as a realignment with Apple's core values and brought meaning and purpose back to the company.[5] While adjusting Apple's hiring philosophy, he famously remarked, "It doesn't make sense to hire smart people and then tell them what to do; we hire smart people so they can tell us what to do."[6]

In essence, Jobs' genius was in recognizing that significant change requires a series of well-thought-out evolutionary steps. Change is an evolution, not a revolution.

Leading and navigating through significant and sustainable change is more art than science. While data and research can guide us toward understanding the nuances of transformation, it's the human touch, intuition, and creativity that truly result in enduring change. Leaders and individuals must manage change with a blend of inspiration and understanding. They act like painters who choose the right colors and strokes to evoke emotion on canvas. They feel the rhythm of the moment, recognize when to push forward and when to pause, and appreciate the unique context in which change unfolds. In this nuanced dance of evolution, the heart and soul often lead the way more effectively than any formula or algorithm.

This is precisely why the shifts needed to live a meaningful life or lead a successful organization are subtle. Like art, these shifts aren't always apparent, and people often struggle to see their utility. As the American Heritage Dictionary says, they are "so slight as to be difficult to detect or describe."[7] They are difficult to understand because, in essence, they are elusive. They are hidden from view and difficult to discern.

In our fast-paced world, where monumental changes and grand gestures often grab the spotlight, the power of these subtle shifts is frequently underestimated. Yet, the quiet, nuanced, almost imperceptible changes usually have the most profound and lasting impacts. Just as a delicate brushstroke can change the entire mood of a painting, a subtle shift in mindset and behavior can set the course for a significant transformation. Though often overlooked, these subtle shifts are the building blocks of sustainable and considerable change. When accumulated over time, they pave the way for a richer, more fulfilling life experience.

Subtle shifts are the building blocks of a successful life and effective leadership, and by looking at them systematically, we can improve our odds of creating intentional and sustainable change.

Here's to making subtle shifts.

Introduction

Imagine yourself on a long, open highway. It's 5:30 AM, and you are heading to the beach for your annual family vacation. The car hums steadily along, and a quiet excitement fills the air. The sky is just beginning to lighten, the kids are asleep, and music plays softly in the background. The road is smooth, there is barely a car in sight, and you're thinking this will be an easy ride. All you have to do is stay in your lane, keep moving forward, and eventually, you'll reach your destination, maybe even a little early.

But have you ever stopped to think about how you get from point A to point B? Keeping a car in its lane isn't a one-time choice. It's a series of barely noticeable actions and minor adjustments that keep you on track. Your hands make subtle adjustments to the steering wheel continuously. Your foot adjusts its pressure slightly on the gas pedal to keep you moving at a certain speed. You quietly move that foot between the gas and the brake without thinking. Your eyes constantly scan the horizon, looking for threats and obstacles, and your brain processes everything quickly, like a complex algorithm, telling your body how to adjust to its immediate surroundings.

The simple act of driving isn't so simple, and the fact that so many people can get from point A to point B without killing themselves is a miracle. Just ask anyone who has been in an accident, and they will tell you how quickly it can all go wrong. Miss those minor adjustments, and you'll start to drift. Ever so slightly at first, but before long, you're skimming the shoulder, maybe even crossing into oncoming traffic.

I use this metaphor with my clients because it captures the real nature of how we can approach our lives and reach our goals. Success doesn't happen in sweeping, life-altering moments or grand overhauls. It's about subtle, steady adjustments that, over time, keep us aligned with where we want to go. Success and progress are a lot like driving a car. Those who successfully get to their destination do so by constantly adapting without us noticing.

The first time I heard this metaphor, something clicked. It hit me that we expect change to feel significant and dramatic, something we can see or measure in real-time. But just like driving, growth rarely works that way. In fact, it's often just the opposite. Real progress is so quiet that we barely notice it happening. Only later, when we look back, do we realize that those minor course corrections added up to something substantial and lasting.

Think about it: as you're driving, those tiny nudges of the wheel don't feel like much. They barely move at all. But let go for a moment, and you'll feel it—the car starts to pull to one side, and soon you're veering off course. It's subtle at first, almost a gentle slide. But the longer you wait, the sharper you'll need to pull back to get on track. What might have been a smooth drive can turn into a jarring correction. And if we let things drift too long, it can feel nearly impossible to get back on course.

That is how personal and professional growth works, too. When we wait for significant, sweeping changes, we drift before we realize it and then find ourselves scrambling to correct, usually making harsh and uncomfortable adjustments to get back to where we started. It's disheartening, sometimes even exhausting. But when we recognize the power of subtle, consistent adjustments—when we keep a light, steady grip and make tiny course corrections along the way—the whole journey changes. What once felt uncertain or chaotic becomes smoother, more intentional, and more sustainable.

This is the real work of transformation. It's not glamorous and doesn't always make for a grand story. But it creates the kind of change that lasts. The difference between veering wildly off course and reaching our destination isn't in the strength of one dramatic shift but in the consistency of those quiet, subtle adjustments that guide us forward.

The transformation treadmill

Every January, I watch the same thing play out at my local gym. The parking lot, which is typically half-empty, suddenly overflows with cars. Inside, the place is packed with newly minted fitness enthusiasts, and every single one has that unmistakable look of resolution in their eyes. These are the New Year's resolutionaries, armed with ambitious goals, unlimited monthly memberships, and visions of turning their lives around by getting back in shape.

But all of this comes to a screeching halt by the middle of February—the parking lot returns to normal. The treadmills stand mostly empty again, and you no longer have to wait for equipment.

The dreamers retreat and surrender to the reality that change is hard work. They become the latest casualties of the transformation treadmill—the exhausting cycle of pursuing dramatic change, burning out, giving up, and starting over again.

Have you ever been on this treadmill? We all experience it at some point, and the pattern is always the same. It starts when you realize something has to change and decide to pursue a seismic shift. You imagine what it would be like to lose thirty pounds in three months, double your department's productivity by quarter's end, or completely reinvent your leadership style so everyone loves you. You make a big, bold commitment to yourself and others, do a bit of research, and jump on the treadmill.

The start is always exciting. You throw yourself into the change with unstoppable enthusiasm. You convince yourself that you will be one of the success stories, one of the few who actually makes it. You suppress any doubts and imagine that this time is different.

Except it isn't.

Like a runner on a treadmill who sets the speed too high, you can maintain the pace for a while through sheer willpower. But eventually, fatigue sets in. The changes you're pursuing are too big and unsustainable. Your energy wanes. Your resolve weakens. The outcome you wanted remains out of reach, and you find yourself right back where you started—only now you're exhausted, discouraged, and convinced that meaningful change is impossible.

Then, after some time, you climb back on the treadmill and start the process all over again.

This endless cycle happens in many domains. It isn't just frustrating—it's expensive. Organizations pour billions into transformation initiatives that fail to deliver lasting results, and

Pursuing significant, dramatic changes quickly exhausts our willpower.

individuals spend countless hours and dollars on self-improvement programs that lead nowhere. The real cost, though, isn't measured in money or time but in the toll it takes on our confidence and capability.

Every failed attempt at dramatic change reinforces our deepest fears about our ability to improve. Each time we fall off the treadmill, we become more convinced that we're the problem. We might not tell anyone this, but we start to believe we lack discipline, commitment, or whatever quality we believe successful people possess. We develop change fatigue and become increasingly cynical about the possibility of even the slightest transformation.

The irony is that while we're running ourselves ragged on the treadmill, we're moving backward. Pursuing significant, dramatic changes quickly exhausts our willpower—a limited resource that, like a muscle, tires out under constant strain, leaving us less capable of sustaining progress. On top of that, significant shifts activate our brain's threat response, shifting control to the amygdala, the fear center, and throwing us into survival mode where creativity and adaptability are stifled. These grand efforts also stir up internal and external resistance, draining energy as we battle doubts, discomfort, and potential pushback from others. And in our rush to make things happen, we often skip the crucial step of understanding the root of our patterns. Without that insight, we're bound to repeat the same cycles—whether in a different gym, a new job, or with the latest self-help strategy—leaving real change out of reach.

As a coach, I've watched this play out with countless clients. Several years ago, I worked with a senior executive named Maria, who was stuck on the transformation treadmill. After receiving feedback that her directive leadership style was hurting team morale, she committed to completely reinventing her approach. She announced to her team that she was turning over a new leaf. She would transform from a commanding leader into a collaborative one—overnight.

For several weeks, Maria pursued her ambitious goal. She sought consensus on every decision, no matter how small. She replaced giving directions with asking questions. She stopped offering direct feedback. Her team appreciated her sudden transformation, but productivity plummeted as simple decisions turned into endless discussions.

Eventually, Maria got frustrated and reverted to her old style—only now with an added layer of resentment and a deeper conviction that she couldn't change. She had fallen into the classic trap of the transformation treadmill: believing that meaningful change requires dramatic reinvention.

What Maria didn't realize—and what most of us don't when we're caught on the treadmill—is that sustainable change rarely comes through revolution. Change happens naturally—it's all about evolution—and the most successful changes often look unimpressive in the moment. They're too small to trigger our threat response, too subtle to exhaust our willpower, and too gradual to generate significant resistance.

This isn't just philosophical theory—it's backed by research. Studies in behavioral science show that small, consistent changes create more lasting results than dramatic overhauls.[1] Neuroscience reveals that tiny adjustments are more likely to rewire neural pathways, fostering long-term behavioral change without activating the brain's threat response.[2] Even organizational psychology researchers tell us that employees are more likely to embrace gradual changes in the workplace, because they generate less resistance and preserve a sense of psychological safety.[3]

Yet we keep climbing back onto the treadmill and cranking up the speed. We seem convinced that if we run a little faster, push a little harder, or hang on a little longer, we'll finally achieve the dramatic transformation we seek. We've become addicted to the illusion of rapid change, even as evidence of its ineffectiveness piles up.

The real tragedy isn't that we fail to achieve dramatic transformation. The real tragedy is that while we're pushing ourselves to the limit on the treadmill, we're missing the true path to lasting change—one that is paved with subtle shifts.

The profound power of subtle shifts

Why do we keep getting on this treadmill? It's simple: we're addicted to the idea of dramatic change. Our culture celebrates overnight success stories, radical reinventions, and big, bold breakthroughs. We watch shows like The Biggest Loser, binge on makeover reveals, and listen to a twenty-four-seven news cycle that dramatizes change. The message is clear but deceiving: if you want real change, it must be big, bold, and dramatic.

Our addiction to dramatic change runs deep. We've convinced ourselves that anything less than a complete overhaul means we aren't serious about change. We're almost disappointed when someone tells us they lost weight by taking the stairs instead of the elevator. We want to hear about their epic battle with weight loss and their dramatic story of stamina and persistence. We want to believe that change is hard.

But here's the thing: while we're stuck in the drama of transformation, we're missing something crucial. The real power to change—the power that actually works—is far less dramatic.

After twenty years of working with leaders and watching countless change attempts fail, I've noticed something interesting. The people who create lasting change rarely do it through dramatic moves. Instead, they make tiny adjustments that add up to remarkable results over time. And these tiny tweaks are often invisible to the naked eye. They are subtle and, therefore elusive. They are far from the obvious targets most of us look to when we want to change.

Think about the leader who pauses for a moment before reacting to bad news, the executive who starts to see mistakes as learning opportunities rather than failures, or the manager who stops trying to prove he has all the answers and starts truly listening to his team. These shifts are so subtle that most people never notice them, but they change everything.

Now, I want to be clear that this book, *Subtle Shifts*, isn't a rehash of the same old concepts, and my intention isn't to put a clever spin on popular personal development concepts. This book isn't the same as *Atomic Habits*, *Tiny Habits*, or other popular approaches to behavior change. While these concepts are valuable and focus on building better habits through small, observable actions, subtle shifts operate at a deeper level and they start before habits. So, what are they?

> **Subtle shifts are small, elusive changes that occur in the mind before they appear in behavior. They transform how we see and understand our world, creating a profound impact through slight adjustments that are often invisible to others.**

Think about the person dedicated to consistently working out at the gym. You might think her discipline and habits get her to the gym, but I suggest otherwise. I believe a subtle shift occurred before she could build the habit. Perhaps it was the moment she stopped seeing exercise as punishment and started viewing it as self-care. Or maybe it was when she shifted from focusing on losing weight to embracing movement as a form of personal expression and joy.

These mental shifts, imperceptible to others, create the foundation for all lasting change. They're the quiet transformations in perspective that precede visible action. While habits shape our behaviors, subtle shifts shape our relationship with those behaviors. They're the difference between forcing yourself to go to the gym and wanting to go to the gym.

I see examples of this all the time in the business world, but years ago, one of my clients had a subtle shift that completely redefined how I looked at change.

Sarah was a brilliant manager and problem solver, but she tended to micromanage her team. That is until one day, her team started falling apart under her leadership. Sarah tried to jump in to fix everything herself, but the stress overcame her, and she started steamrolling others. Thankfully, her boss saw what was happening and decided to get her some help.

After several conversations with Sarah, we realized that the real issue wasn't merely her behaviors—it was where she placed her attention. She was hyper-focused on results and saw every interaction as a transaction to move projects forward. In her drive to deliver, she'd lost sight of the relationships that make results possible and failed to develop others.

While habits shape our behaviors, subtle shifts shape our relationship with those behaviors.

Once Sarah learned to shift her attention between results and relationships, everything started to change. She didn't become a different person by any stretch of the imagination, but Sarah softened her rough edges. Her relationships improved, collaboration increased, and her leadership effectiveness scores increased—all because of a shift in attention so subtle that most people, including her boss, probably couldn't pinpoint exactly what had changed.

Another client, Bob, had a similar experience. As a construction executive, Bob was always tough and decisive. He was plagued with black-and-white thinking and quick judgments, and he had no room for grey areas. This worked for years until it didn't. The CEO grew frustrated with him, his team started avoiding him, and at home, his kids stopped talking to him.

When I started working with Bob, others told me he needed to make dramatic changes. They wanted him to change his leadership style, executive presence, attitude, and communications. But those surface-level issues weren't really the problem. What Bob needed to change were his assumptions about leadership.

During coaching conversations, Bob began questioning and shifting his assumptions about what made a good leader. We discussed his roles and responsibilities extensively and explored alternative perspectives on leadership. Then, one day, it clicked. He realized he needed to let go of his desire to control, and he started listening instead of jumping to conclusions. Within months, everyone noticed a different leader in Bob. People were amazed at his transformation but couldn't quite explain what had changed.

The change was nothing earth-shattering. Bob didn't undergo a personality transplant or a dramatic attitude adjustment. He also didn't set out to make a huge habit or behavior change. He simply made a few subtle shifts in what he believed about leadership, and the shifts paid dividends. Within months, his leadership effectiveness scores shot up by 20%, and his team started to enjoy working with him. And, as a bonus, his kids started to open up to him again, and Bob felt better than he had in years.

So, what can we learn from Sarah and Bob? Change isn't about dramatic moves around obvious things. It's about slight adjustments to subtle things that create the leverage to change. Think of it like tuning a guitar. The adjustments are so slight you can barely see them, but that tiny turn of the tuning key sets you up to play beautiful music that others enjoy. This isn't just easier than dramatic change—it's more effective. Small shifts work because they become part of who we are rather than something we have to force. They work with our nature instead of against it.

This might sound too simple. In a world of "transform your life in thirty days" promises, saying "make tiny adjustments" or "trust the process" isn't very sexy. But it works. And at the end of the day, that's what matters when it comes to change.

How this book will help you

This book is here to help you step off the transformation treadmill and make real, meaningful progress in your life. Rather than feeling stuck, stressed, and scattered, you'll find a new sense of freedom, focus, and flow. Through the power of subtle shifts, you'll learn how to create growth without the exhaustion that comes from chasing dramatic, unsustainable change.

These subtle adjustments act like small hinges that swing big doors, setting off a chain reaction that builds resilience, adaptability, and clarity across every area of your life. By refining where you focus your attention, challenging limiting assumptions, and adjusting your actions in small but significant ways, you'll find yourself living and leading with more clarity and confidence, and inspiring others through your example. I hope this book will guide you to achieve lasting, authentic growth, help you reclaim your energy, and create the impact you've always wanted—on your terms.

How this book is structured

This book will help you think differently about change, how you change yourself, and how you lead change. It will help you become a better person and a better leader. I wrote this book because, after three decades working with high achievers, I've seen too many talented people burn out trying to force dramatic transformations. This book offers a better way.

The path to lasting change isn't paved with dramatic overhauls but with subtle shifts in three areas—attention, assumptions, and actions. Think of these dimensions as three dials that unlock a safe. When you learn to make subtle adjustments to each dial—shifting where you focus your attention, what you believe to be true, and how you show up in the world—you unlock your identity, productivity, and maturity as a leader.

The diagram below shows how these three dimensions fit together. Keep this diagram in mind as you read; it will help you see how small adjustments in each area combine to create remarkable results.

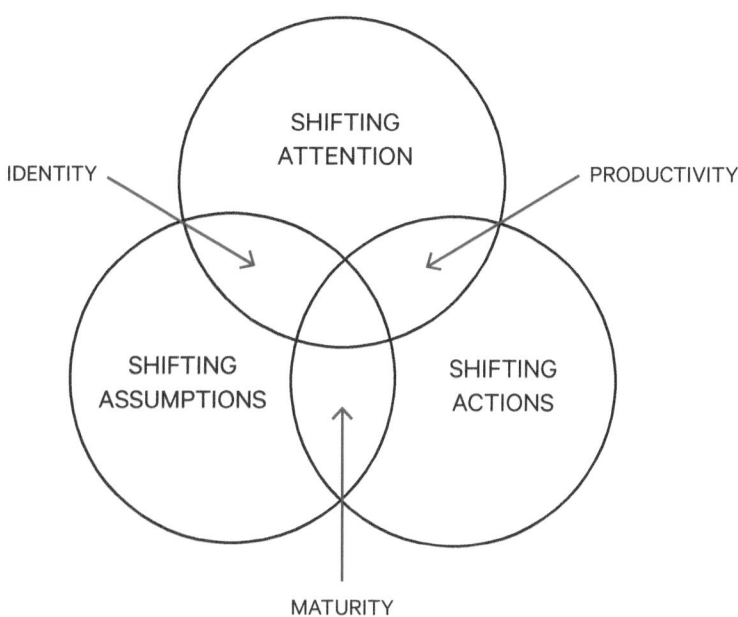

PART ONE: SHIFTING ATTENTION

Your attention is a powerful force that determines everything you do and accomplish. Like a magnet is drawn toward true north, your attention draws forth your achievements. Focusing attention has become a rare and valuable skill in today's fast-paced, information-rich world. In this section, I'll teach you how to shift your attention toward the things that matter most so you can enhance your effectiveness and lead with more purpose and integrity.

We'll begin by learning to *Evaluate* attention. The key here is to expand your awareness and recognize where your attention is at any given moment. By observing and understanding your current focus, you'll gain valuable insights into your priorities and how they align with your aspirations.

Next, you'll learn to *Eliminate* the distracting desires that continuously capture your attention. By identifying and letting go of those distractions, you'll free up mental and emotional energy to focus on what truly matters and enhance your ability to pursue your most meaningful goals with clarity and conviction.

Finally, you'll discover how to *Elevate* your attention and focus on your highest priorities. This will help you stay out of the weeds and unlock new levels of success, fulfillment, and meaning for yourself and the people you lead.

PART TWO: SHIFTING ASSUMPTIONS

Once you can control your attention, it's time to focus on shifting assumptions. Here, you'll discover why your thoughts and beliefs influence your results. I'll show you how to challenge and reframe these assumptions to create profound changes in your leadership effectiveness.

In this section, you'll learn to *Contemplate* and think about your thinking. We'll discuss why you must take the time to listen to your inner wisdom and guide your attention back to what truly matters. Through contemplation, you'll foster a deeper connection with your authentic self and find ways to operate with more integrity.

Then we'll talk about how important it is to *Collaborate*. I'll explain how others influence our assumptions and suggest ways to expand your perspective.

And finally, I'll help you *Update* your assumptions and integrate them into your day-to-day actions so you can be more effective as a leader. I'll introduce twelve assumptions that tend to hold leaders back and suggest ways to replace those assumptions with more empowering beliefs.

PART THREE: SHIFTING ACTIONS

With your attention and assumptions in check, we'll explore how you can shift your actions. Action is an important part of the process because the choices you make determine whether subtle shifts will lead to lasting impact.

First, we will *Formulate* strategies that are aligned with your goals and flexible enough to adapt to changing circumstances. I'll guide you through a strategic thinking process and help you craft clear, actionable, and adaptive strategies. By learning to formulate effective strategies, you'll be better equipped to navigate the complexities of leadership and steer your team or organization toward success.

Next, we'll *Calibrate* your actions to ensure they perfectly align with your strategic objectives. This involves regularly assessing your actions and making necessary adjustments to stay on course. I'll provide practical tools and questions to help you continuously calibrate your actions, ensuring you consistently move in the right direction and avoid pitfalls.

Finally, I'll teach you to *Navigate* challenges by finding the sweet spot in every situation. Navigating requires noticing when you aren't at your best and choosing appropriate actions. I'll teach you how to identify and operate from the sweet spot, allowing you to lead with greater agility, resilience, and confidence as you guide your team through change and uncertainty.

Throughout this book, you'll meet people I've coached who successfully applied these strategies and the subtle shifts within them. I've changed all client names and identifiable details to protect their privacy, but the stories remain true to their experiences. I'll provide detailed accounts of how subtle shifts resulted in sustainable success for my clients and their teams, and you'll discover how you can do the same.

At the end of each chapter, I'll summarize key points you can apply in your life. Be sure to make note of the critical points and use them along the way. They're designed to accelerate your growth and achievement.

Say goodbye to the days of feeling stuck and ineffective in leadership and life. Stop second-guessing yourself as you struggle to inspire others and create meaningful, sustainable change. It's time for a new, subtle system for change, and this book will show you how.

PART 1

Shifting Attention

ONE

Evaluate: Pay Attention to Your Attention

"These days cry out, as never before, for us to pay attention, so we can move through them and get our joy and pride back."
~ Anne Lamott

When you were young, did anyone ever tell you to pay attention? I feel like this was a constant phrase in my life, and even though I was never diagnosed with ADHD (Attention Deficit Hyperactivity Disorder), I wonder if I have a mild version of it. Paying attention was never a strong suit for me, and as I grew older, I realized my attention wandered around like a puppy in a room full of squirrels.

I guess that's why I spent so much of my career obsessed with time management and productivity systems. I always wanted to be successful, but my attention seemed to always let me down.

Our goals and systems rest on the fragile foundation of attention.

Since I always felt scattered, I looked to systems and structures to compensate. I wanted to work around my wandering mind and thought a clever system would do the trick.

David Allen's *Getting Things Done*, Michael Hyatt's *Free To Focus*, Peter Bregman's *18 Minutes*, and James Clear's *Atomic Habits* all hold prominent spaces on my bookshelves. These wonderful books provided the structure I desperately needed. I attribute much of my success to what I learned from these authors. I honestly don't think I could have succeeded in my career without their advice. But after implementing what they taught me and struggling to make it all work, I realized something was missing.

Productivity systems, time management strategies, and habits are exciting concepts, but like everything, they are incomplete. Please don't take this as criticism; I mean it when I say everything is incomplete, and I know this book is no exception. Productivity systems, time management strategies, and atomic habits only work if you can focus on them; therefore, attention is a prerequisite.

James Clear famously writes in *Atomic Habits*, "You do not rise to the level of your goals. You fall to the level of your systems."[1] I agree with him, but I'd argue that there is more to this concept. Our goals and systems rest on the fragile foundation of attention; therefore, our attention deserves our attention. If our attention is shaky, our systems will crumble like a house of cards. Attention is a critical foundation for the success of most systems, and we need to learn to make subtle shifts in our attention if we want sustainable success.

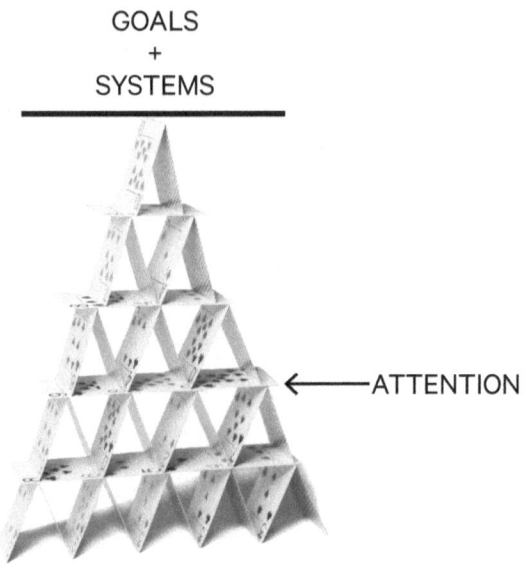

Where is your attention?

What are you paying attention to? Right now, where is your attention? Are you focused on the words on this page, or is your mind drifting elsewhere? And if it's drifting, where is it going?

If you're like many of us, you're quite self-aware; you likely wouldn't be reading this if you weren't. And with this self-awareness, you'll likely agree that your attention often strays, a common hurdle in our fast-paced era. Let's be honest: in our modern world, attention is a precious commodity, more scarce and fragmented than ever. The rapid pace of technological progress and the ubiquity of digital media have turned our attention into a battleground, with various stimuli competing for it in every waking moment.

Consider this: the average person receives about sixty-three phone notifications every day.[2] That's sixty-three interruptions, sixty-three potential shifts in focus, and sixty-three opportunities for your attention to be hijacked. Can you remember the last time you had an uninterrupted hour free from the ping of a notification or the urge to check your email?

However, external interruptions are only part of the problem. Our internal environment is just as cluttered. A study published by Harvard professors Matthew Killingsworth and Daniel Gilbert found that people spend almost 47% of their waking hours thinking about something other than what they're doing.[3] Why? Mind wandering is hard-wired into our brains. It's no wonder everyone is obsessed with paying attention.

To make matters worse, mind wandering is a significant barrier to happiness and productivity. Our attention is a limited resource, and it stresses us out when we try to focus too hard on something. The brain wants to wander and think about what is not happening, which dilutes our focus and diminishes our ability to pay attention.

When mind wandering becomes an accepted habit, we justify it by telling ourselves that we need to multitask, but multitasking creates other problems. It leads to scattered focus and shallow results, and one study found that it can lower our IQ by as much as ten points.[4] Just to put the IQ drop in perspective, this is twice the amount found in studies on the impact of smoking marijuana.

Like using drugs, misusing our attention is highly problematic. You will pay the price if you try to do multiple things simultaneously. Sure, you can watch TV while scrolling through your phone, check emails during meetings, and think about work while eating dinner with your family, but you'll pay the price. The consequences of scattered attention are real, and it is time to recognize that life isn't just a matter of efficiency; it's about the quality of engagement with the world around us.

The multitasking myth

The allure of multitasking and constant connectivity is understandable. We live in a society that glorifies busy-ness and productivity. The more you do, the more you're worth, or so the story goes. But as we try to do more, we lose our ability to do things that matter, and the irony is profound. By trying to do it all, we end up achieving very little.

Research consistently shows that our attention has limits. A study by Kep Kee Loh and Ryota Kanai from the University of Sussex found that individuals who engage in heavy multitasking have less brain density in the anterior cingulate cortex, a region responsible for impulse control and decision-making.[5] Another revealing statistic comes from Stanford University, where researchers discovered that chronic multitaskers are worse at organizing their thoughts, filtering out irrelevant information, and shifting between tasks efficiently.[6]

The consequences of buying into the multitasking myth are far-reaching. It leads to lower quality and productivity, harms our mental health, and reduces our ability to engage deeply and meaningfully with tasks, people, and even our thoughts.

In his book *Four Thousand Weeks*, Oliver Burkeman aptly captures the essence of this issue. He writes, "Productivity is a trap. Becoming more efficient just makes you more rushed, and trying to clear the decks simply makes them fill up again faster. Nobody in the history of humanity has ever achieved 'work-life balance', whatever that might be, and you certainly won't get there by copying the 'six things successful people do before 7:00 AM.' The day will never arrive when you finally have everything under control."[7] Burkeman points out the folly of trying to do everything—in trying to capture every opportunity, we squander our finite time.

The multitasking myth is seductive because it promises us control over time, tasks, and productivity. But it delivers the opposite. By scattering our attention across multiple fronts, we lose control over our most valuable resource: our attention.

Taking back control

The biggest obstacle in our quest to manage attention is a lack of self-awareness. No one ever thinks they lack self-awareness, but as we move through the day with a constant barrage of distractions, it slips further and further away from us. As our attention migrates from one distraction to another, we lose our sense of true north and struggle to find our bearings. Like a hiker lost in the woods without a map and compass, we operate on instinct, do whatever it takes to survive, and fall into a reactive state where self-awareness is lost.

But this reactive state can be avoided if we pause momentarily to regain control. The act of pausing is a subtle shift in *action* that can create a subtle shift in *attention*. Ask yourself the following questions to evaluate where your attention is anchored and reclaim control of your attention.

AM I FOCUSING ON CONTENT OR CONTEXT?

Picture this: You're at your desk, buried under a mountain of paperwork, emails pinging every other minute, and your phone buzzing like it's on a caffeine high. That's the content part of your day—the tasks, the to-dos, the endless checklist of things demanding your attention. It's like being in the middle of a bustling city street, with honks and shouts, and the hustle and bustle engulfing you. Then the context comes in—it's like stepping into a hot air balloon floating a mile above the city. Suddenly, you're in a space where you can see the bigger picture.

Focusing on content alone is like trying to understand a movie by watching a single scene. Sure, you might understand the gist of what is happening, but you miss the storyline, the character development, and the plot twists. The context is the movie in its entirety. It's understanding not just what you're doing but why you're doing it. It's the difference between watching scenes from a movie in random order and watching the entire film from start to finish.

In the workplace, it's easy to get caught up in day-to-day tasks and lose sight of your organization's overall mission and goals. When you're solely content-focused, you might excel at ticking off tasks but fail to align your efforts with your company's broader strategy. You become the worker bee who's busy but not necessarily effective.

Contextual focus is very different. When we focus on context, we begin to understand how our work fits into the bigger picture. We start to recognize the impact of our actions on our team, our organization, and even on ourselves. It involves asking questions like: "How does this task advance our collective goals?", "How does this align with our values?", or "What's the larger purpose behind this project?"

Focusing on context helps you to prioritize. Not all tasks are created equal, and understanding their larger context lets you decide what needs immediate attention and what can wait. It's the art of discerning the urgent from the important, the trivial from the significant.

This dichotomy plays out in our personal lives, too. Focusing solely on the content of your day—the chores, the errands, the appointments—can make life seem like a never-ending to-do list.

But when you step back and look at the context—your relationships, your goals, your values—suddenly, those tasks have meaning. They're no longer just chores; they're the building blocks of the life you're creating.

The content of your day is unavoidable, but the context gives it meaning. Balancing these two is not just a skill but an art. It's about finding that sweet spot where you're not just doing things right but doing the right things.

Here's a practical tip. Next time you're drowning in the sea of content, pause and ask yourself: "Am I balancing my attention across content and context?" The answer might be the life raft you need.

AM I FOCUSED ON RESULTS OR RELATIONSHIPS?

In today's world, where everyone seems to be keeping score, it's easy to get fixated on outcomes. We look at results and outcomes as the sine qua non of success, and anticipated results capture our attention. But here's a thought: what if we shifted our focus from the finish line to the people running alongside us? That's the essence of this subtle shift in attention.[8]

Let's face it: we're often told that success is measured in tangible achievements and encouraged to be results-focused. We are told to begin with the end in mind, plan our work and work our plan, and measure our success with clock-like precision. This results-focused approach is like being a marathon runner focusing only on the finish line. You might cross it first or achieve a personal record, but what's the point if you've elbowed everyone else out of the way to get there?

Success today is about so much more than achieving an outcome. People care deeply about how you achieve the things you achieve. A "take no prisoners" approach or bulldozing your way to the top has consequences. Society benefits from pursuing a higher standard of success that values how you do what you do as much or even more than what you do.

Think about a leader you worked for who left a lasting positive impression on you. Or think about that person in your life you admire and look up to. What did you admire about this person? I've asked hundreds of people this question, and the answers are almost always the same. People don't remember the list of achievements. They remember the way that person made them feel. They admire how that person showed up.

Successful people understand that results are fleeting, and relationships endure, so they work hard to shift their attention from one to the other and then back again. They don't get stuck focusing all their attention on results; likewise, they don't use it all up on relationships. They pivot back and forth between the two and enjoy the best of both worlds. Essentially, they create results with and through other people.

So, here's a practical tip: next time you're zeroed in on a result, take a moment to connect with others. Tell them what you are up to and ask about their lives. Step away from the relentless pursuit of results to connect and build relationships, and you will find that it pays dividends. You can find meaningful and sustainable success by shifting your attention between results and relationships.

AM I FOCUSED ON OBSTACLES OR OPPORTUNITIES?

Imagine you're on a hike, moving through a trail cluttered with fallen trees, slick rocks, and steep hills. Where does your focus go? If you only see the hazards, that hike turns into a grind, with all your attention on the next step. But if you're open to what's around you—the challenge, the chance to build strength, the friend walking beside you—that same hike feels entirely different. Obstacles or opportunities? It's a choice we get to make.

This shift isn't just for the trail; it's essential in all walks of life. Business is full of obstacles: conflict, competition, and unpredictable markets. If we lock onto those, the job feels like a constant uphill battle, exhausting and limited. But asking, "What can I gain from this?" or "Where's the opportunity here?" changes the story. A project falling behind could be a chance to strengthen teamwork, retool processes, or identify inefficiencies. The obstacle doesn't change—but how we approach it does. And that shift, even slightly, opens up entirely new options.

This mindset shift matters in our personal lives, too. We all face setbacks in our relationships, communities, and hobbies. We get stuck if we see these as problems and fixate on them. But reframing them as opportunities can change the game. That's where growth comes in. Losing a job might be the push to pursue something meaningful. A challenging moment in a relationship might improve communication or bring you closer. A health issue might inspire a new way of living or a move to a nicer climate.

Let's be honest, though: shifting our attention from obstacles to opportunities isn't easy. Some of us seem hardwired to notice what is broken, while others are walking bundles of optimism. The trick is to be conscious of your tendencies and realize you can choose where to focus your attention. This conscious choice is your power—your control over your narrative. If you choose to look at the obstacles, that will serve you well in one circumstance; if you choose to look at the opportunities, that will serve you well in another.

Neither is inherently better, and both are appropriate depending on the circumstances.

So, next time you're up against a challenge, pause to ask, "What obstacles are in front of me?" and "What opportunity does this obstacle present?" If you can ask these questions in stressful times, you'll improve your ability to shift your attention and alter how you show up.

AM I FOCUSED INWARD OR OUTWARD?

In the theater of life, where we are both the audience and the actors, our focus often oscillates between the internal and the external—the self and the world around us. This dichotomy raises a critical question: "Am I focused inward or outward?" In other words, "Am I focused on myself or on others?" Understanding this balance is essential because we will struggle to perform if we focus too much on ourselves.

Let's consider the inward focus first. It's reflective and centered on our thoughts, feelings, and personal experiences. While self-reflection is crucial, excessive inward focus can veer into ego-driven territory. It's like looking into a mirror; it's beneficial for self-examination, but if you stare too long, you risk becoming Narcissus, enamored with your reflection. Self-absorption can blind you to the needs and experiences of others, creating a bubble of self-centeredness.

At work, it might manifest as a relentless drive for personal achievement without regard for team dynamics. In our personal lives, it can lead to strained relationships, as focusing on self eclipses the mutual give-and-take that nourishes connections.

Now, let's shift our attention outward. Focusing outward is about pointing the lens towards others and the world around us. It's service-driven, marked by empathy, compassion, and a genuine interest in the well-being of others.

In the workplace, an outward focus translates into collaborative efforts, where the team's success precedes individual accolades. It's about creating value not just for yourself but for the organization and its stakeholders. In your personal life, it strengthens relationships, as it involves actively listening, understanding, and responding to the needs and feelings of others.

But here's the catch: it's not about choosing one over the other. It's not either/or. Life isn't a zero-sum game where focusing on others means neglecting yourself. The real magic lies in striking a balance. It's about being self-aware without being self-absorbed and being considerate without losing oneself in the process.

Think of it as a two-way street. By focusing outward, you gain insights and perspectives that enrich your inward focus. Conversely, a healthy inward focus allows you to engage more authentically and meaningfully with the world. It's a symbiotic relationship where one feeds into the other.

Take action

Ask these four questions whenever you want to shift your attention. The questions aren't exhaustive, but they function as trigger points to help us shift our attention to meet our circumstances. If you don't pay attention to your attention and consciously choose where to place it, you'll never be able to navigate toward the goals you

Ask four questions to shift your attention.

are pursuing. Asking these questions whenever your attention is scattered will help you get back on track.

Here's a practical tip: start each day by setting an intention to balance your focus. Pair every inward-looking goal or activity with an outward-focused one. It could be as simple as following up a self-reflection session with an act of kindness toward someone else. By achieving this balance, we enrich not only our own lives but also the lives of those around us.

Chapter Summary

- If you want to shift your attention, pay attention to your attention. It is a dynamic, scattered, and finite resource that needs careful management.

- Scattered attention can lead to severe consequences, including missed opportunities, professional setbacks, and personal turmoil.

- Multitasking does not enhance productivity; it destroys it. It spreads your attention thinly across tasks, leading to lower-quality work, increased stress, and reduced effectiveness.

- Taking control of your attention starts with self-awareness. Pausing and reflecting on where your attention is anchored is essential to reclaiming focus and direction in personal and professional contexts.

- There are four key questions when evaluating attention: Am I focused on content or context? Results or relationships? Obstacles or opportunities? Inward or outward?

- Balancing attention between these opposites is crucial. By consciously choosing where to place your attention, you can navigate towards your goals more effectively, enrich your experiences, and improve both your work and relationships.

TWO

Eliminate: Discard Distracting Desires

"Happiness can only be found if you can free yourself of all other distractions."
~ Saul Bellow

Remember Anakin Skywalker? He was the young Jedi hopeful-turned Sith Lord in the Star Wars movies.[1] He started as a skilled, well-meaning Jedi with loads of potential. But Anakin wasn't focused on saving the galaxy. He was focused on himself and possessed some troubling traits. He craved power, feared loss, wanted control, and sought love, which eventually turned him into the villain we've come to know as Darth Vader.

But have you ever stopped to consider that Anakin's story isn't just a tale from a galaxy far, far away? It reflects what many experience today, and like Anakin, we are constantly bombarded with temptations. We are promised the treasures of wealth, knowledge, power, and control, and are inundated with marketing messages that promise the world. We are told we can have it all with little to no consequence, and we are convinced that we deserve it all. This leads us to a place where we feel entitled and worthy of the luxuries we see on TV and the reality shows that aren't even real. And before you know it, you are stuck in a tornado of aspirations and desires that tug on our attention, direct us off our path, and create chaos in our lives and workplaces.

Instead of living a life in the present and being grateful for what we have, we accidentally squander it all away. No matter how ridiculous, every little craving captures our time and attention, and distracts us from our true path and calling. And just like the Jedi knights who do all they can to overcome the dark side of The Force, we become blind to the forces at play and surprised by the devastation they bring.

Desire's downside

Desire is a driving force behind humanity's greatest achievements. Without it, we wouldn't have walked on two legs, built societies, or set foot on the moon. But while desire has shaped history, it also has a darker side—it can be addictive and lead us astray.

Desires make us feel good, and satisfying them feels even better. Yet, some desires—especially those that promise immediate gratification and effortless achievement—can be dangerous. In today's whirlwind of constant information and flashy advertisements, our desires often spiral out of control, pulling us away from our true selves and the things that matter most. The lesson from Anakin's fall is clear: mindlessly chasing distracting desires holds us back from reaching our full potential. To grow and thrive, we must learn to

Mindlessly chasing distracting desires holds us back.

identify and discard the desires that derail us and confront the three key challenges they create.

CHALLENGE #1: PARALYZED BY POSSIBILITY

When we juggle too many desires, we end up paralyzed by possibility. Imagine winding down after a long day. You pick up your phone, scroll through social media, and see your friends flaunting vacations, new businesses, and luxury cars. Suddenly, your accomplishments seem small. You've wanted a new car for years, and the desire kicks in like a fire fed with gasoline. Maybe you should buy one this weekend.

Later, as you relax in front of the TV, you see more car commercials and that same car your friend just bought. Your desire grows even more potent. You're convinced: this weekend, you'll make it happen.

But by the time the weekend comes, reality sets in. You spent hours researching the car, but now your spouse is upset because you didn't make time for the family. You feel guilty because the week's priorities slipped through your fingers. Drowning in frustration, you realize you've neglected the things that matter most because you were paralyzed by possibility.

CHALLENGE #2: TOO MANY COMPETING PRIORITIES

The second downside of desire is that it leads to competing priorities. As a coach, I see this in ambitious leaders overwhelmed by too many desires, pulling them in different directions. We believe we should have it all, but one desire replaces another, and soon, we're juggling more than we can handle. If we're not careful, we lose sight of which desires are real and which are distractions.

Take Julie, for example. When she started working in her Fortune 500 company, she worked tirelessly to climb the corporate ladder. Julie believed that reaching the executive level would make her happy. But once she got there, the fulfillment was fleeting. She realized that what she wanted came with many things she didn't want, and the weight of it all was unbearable. It wasn't quite what she expected, and soon, she felt empty, realizing she had been chasing the wrong goals.

CHALLENGE #3: DESIRE CAN LEAD US ASTRAY

Desire can often lead us down the wrong path. Carl, the brilliant founder of a tech startup, worked his butt off but never learned to cope with the stress. He began drinking alcohol to unwind after long days, but the habit of having a glass of wine or a beer after work turned into something far more troubling. His desire for a temporary escape became a dependency that consumed his thoughts and derailed his career. His desire for a temporary escape ultimately cost him his company and the life he had worked so hard to build.

The allure of desire is powerful, but without awareness, it can pull us away from what truly matters. To reach our full potential, we must learn to discern between desires that propel us forward and those that lead us astray—and have the courage to let go of the distractions.

Developing discernment

Like Anakin, many of us are confronted with desires that seem worth pursuing at first glance. This abundance creates a dilemma, not of right versus wrong, but of right versus right. This concept was eloquently proposed by the brilliant ethicist Rushworth Kidder.[2] He believed that the most challenging decisions we make are those where we choose between two mutually exclusive and fundamentally sound paths. That is precisely the challenge we face with our many desires. Each desire, in isolation, may seem positive and worthy of pursuit, but together, they create a cacophony that drowns out our ability to discern our true path.

Imagine your desires as a chorus of voices, each singing a different tune. One voice sings of professional success, another of adventure and exploration, a third of family and friendships, and so on. Individually, each song is beautiful and compelling, but together, they clash. When one voice conflicts with the others, we must choose which to turn off and which to amplify. We can't simply harmonize these distracting desires. If they are distractions that disrupt life's symphony, we must consciously choose to turn them off.

In essence, we need to make difficult choices. If we want to be successful in any endeavor, we need to discern which desires to follow and which to let go of. If we don't, we will end up like Anakin Skywalker who succumbed to his darker desires, and turned away from his noble path. Discernment is necessary if we want to experience life's richer, more fulfilling aspects and pursue our true calling. When we scatter our attention across too many desires, we dilute the intensity and quality of our experience. We minimize our ability to make great choices, making it harder to move forward with purpose and clarity.

We must cultivate discernment to navigate the many desires vying for our attention.

The cost of cognitive load

Pay attention to your cognitive load if you want to be more discerning. Cognitive load is a fancy term for the mental strain we feel when trying to juggle too much information or complex tasks at once.

Just as a computer can only process so many tasks simultaneously before it slows down or crashes, our brains have a finite capacity for processing information. This limitation plays a critical role in navigating our world, particularly in an age where distractions are ubiquitous and our attention is under attack.

Research suggests that the average person checks their phone dozens of times each day, with roughly half of these checks happening during work hours.[3] No matter how brief, these interruptions fragment our attention and add to our cognitive load. This constant switching, driven by the desire to stay connected, can reduce our mental efficiency and productivity. A study by Gloria Mark at the University of California, Irvine, found that it takes an average of 23 minutes and 15 seconds to return to the original task after an interruption.[4] Imagine the cumulative impact of these interruptions on a day's work!

The cost of cognitive overload extends beyond mere productivity. It can have profound implications for our well-being and mental health. The barrage of information and choices that confront us daily can lead to decision fatigue, a psychological phenomenon in which the quality of our decisions deteriorates after a lengthy decision-making session. This explains why, after a long day of work inundated with emails, meetings, and choices, we might need help to make simple decisions like what to cook for dinner or which movie to watch.

Another telling statistic comes from a study on smartphone usage, which found that the average smartphone user touches their phone 2,617 times daily, including every tap, swipe, and scroll.[5] No matter how brief, each interaction is a diversion of attention, a slight cognitive load that adds to a significant mental burden over a day.

The cost of cognitive overload extends beyond mere productivity.

This constant demand for attention can lead to chronic cognitive overload, where our brains perpetually try to keep up with the tasks and information they encounter throughout the day.

Now, let's link this back to discarding distracting desires. In a world where technology and information constantly tax our cognitive resources, discerning and discarding unnecessary desires becomes crucial. Eliminating desires and tasks that do not align with our core values and long-term goals can reduce our cognitive load and free up our attention.

Think of it as decluttering your mind. Just as decluttering a physical space can lead to a more serene and efficient environment, decluttering our cognitive space can lead to clearer thinking, better decision-making, and increased focus. It allows us to direct our limited cognitive resources toward the things that truly matter, enhancing our productivity and ability to find joy and fulfillment in our daily lives.

So, how do we decide which desires to nurture and which to let go of? It starts with an honest exploration of what you really want.

What do you really want

What are your deepest desires, and what do you truly want? If you are like most people, this question can be quite confronting because you want many things. Questioning your desires isn't an everyday, run-of-the-mill activity. It feels unnecessary because we live in a world that promises instant gratification and suggests we can have it all.

I guess this is why discernment is so tricky. Why should we waste our precious time and attention thinking about such things? Even if we are convinced, how should we go about it?

Remember the advice I gave you in Chapter One. You have to evaluate where your attention is going. I have a simple framework you can use to see how your desires capture your attention. Here's how it works.

Take a minute to draw a line from north to south on a piece of paper. At the southern point of the line, write the word concrete. At the northern end of the line, write the word abstract. This line represents two different types of desires.

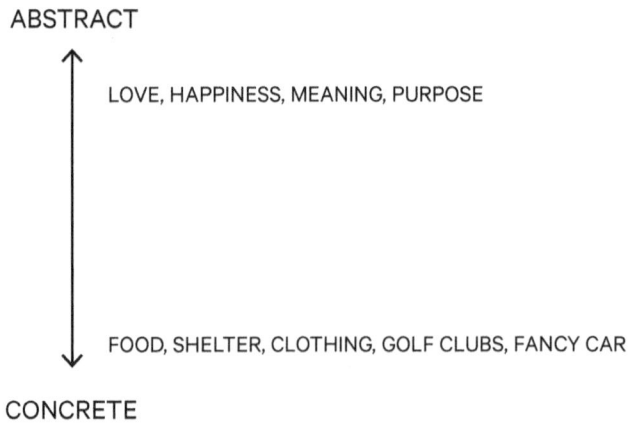

Concrete desires are practical, material, and grounded. They include many things like clothing, food, money, a bigger house, a fancy car, golf clubs, or a book you want to read. These are the hallmarks of success defined by a material world, and on the surface, they seem to promise satisfaction and fulfillment. They are practical things that we think we need in order to reach our abstract desires.

Abstract desires, on the other hand, are conceptual, elusive, and subtle. They include love, happiness, meaning, purpose, fulfillment, and much more. They are less about having and more about being. They reflect our values and point to the essence of who we truly are.

Here's the interesting thing about this exercise: if you take the time to map your desires along this spectrum, you'll likely discover far more concrete desires than abstract ones. Concrete desires often dominate because we have an insidious habit of accumulating them over time. Many people believe that fulfilling concrete desires will clear the path to abstract ones, but nothing could be further from the truth. Accumulating more doesn't produce what we hope it will; instead, it scatters our attention and keeps us from achieving what we want most.

Connecting with the True You

Several years ago, I realized that the desires on the northern point of our diagram are the desires that matter most. I also discovered that they are harder to achieve because they are subtle, nuanced, elusive, and challenging to identify. They reside in a place that I call the True You. This place is difficult to find because it already exists within you but is hidden from view. Let me explain.

In 2014, I attended a leadership conference in Washington, DC, and was excited to see the keynote address of a brilliant executive coach named Doug Silsbee. The stage was empty, apart from a table with a large bell on it. When Doug stepped on stage, he said nothing. He entered from the left, slowly approached the table, pulled out a small hammer, and struck the bell gently. A resonating tone filled the room as Doug stood there in silence. As we waited in anticipation for what seemed like several minutes, Doug peered off into the distance without saying a word. When the sound faded, he struck the bell again, letting the silence linger even longer. It was almost unbearable. I remember sitting there, with a brewing mix of confusion and curiosity, wondering, "What the hell is this guy doing?"

After what felt like an eternity, Doug broke the silence with a very short monologue about the power of pausing. He said that many of us never take the time to pause because we are addicted to action. He suggested that pausing can be one of the most difficult things to do in our busy world and then he quietly asked: "As the vibration moved throughout the room, what did you notice?" He then led the audience through a reflective experience that was powerful and profound; one I will never forget.

As Doug explained our experience, he asked if our minds were filled with thoughts and feelings as the bell vibrated. He suggested that many of us may have felt uncomfortable or curious and asked us to probe deeper into those emotions. He asked us to question where our thoughts and emotions came from and suggested that they came from the egoic self. He explained that the ego, with all its thoughts and feelings, was only a part of us and did not fully represent who we truly were. He challenged us to look beyond the ego, and encouraged us to listen to what I've come to know as the True You.[6]

The True You is hard to explain, but it's an idea that has stood the test of time. It is what Christians call the soul and Muslims call the ruh. It is the divine spirit that lives within all of us and may be the source of life itself. The Quran describes it as God's own spirit that was blown into Adam. In Judaism, they call it neshamah and believe it is the divine breath or spark within each and every person. The idea clearly has legs.

I believe the True You is what Socrates pointed us toward when he urged us to know ourselves. I also believe that when the Buddha spoke of transcending earthly attachments to connect with a more

Your dependable
desires come
from the
True You.

profound sense of self, he was telling us to connect with the true you. Even modern thinkers like Carl Jung have explored this concept and suggested that a collective unconscious existed beyond the ego.[7]

These ancient and modern teachings all point towards a common truth that can help us discard distracting desires. By learning to differentiate between the True You and the ego, we can remain steady amidst the ever-changing desires and thoughts that clutter our daily existence. Your dependable desires come from the True You, and they are untouched by the fleeting whims of surface-level wants.

But here is the challenge: much of this guidance is abstract, ethereal, and out of reach for most people. It's one thing to read about these concepts in philosophical texts or hear them in inspirational talks, but quite another to integrate them into our lives. How can you move beyond the ego and connect with the True You? How can you tell the difference between your egoic desires and your divine desires? You can learn to do so by paying attention to the ego's four core cravings.

The four core cravings

The ego is the guardian of our identity. It protects us psychologically by creating a sense of self. It has a relentless desire to assert itself, and it does so in tricky and troubling ways. One of its most deceptive methods is to convince us that we need something we don't have. Once we take the bait, the ego reels us in like a fish caught on a hook.

If we want to live our lives free from the ego, we must understand how it works. We must recognize it for what it is and know that the ego functions like a craving machine, constantly seeking and yearning for something to soothe and validate it. It's an endless cycle of passion and fulfillment that can trap us in superficial pursuits, leaving little room for genuine self-discovery and growth.

To break free from this cycle, we must learn to recognize these cravings and their role in our daily decisions and interactions. This awareness is the first step towards gaining control over them, allowing us to make choices driven by our values rather than our ego's fleeting desires.

As a craving machine, the ego serves up an array of desires, but four core cravings are worth noting.[8] If we want to shift our attention and live happier, healthier lives, we must see the cravings for what they are—ego-driven desires that can hurt us if they are on overdrive. The four cravings are the desire for control, the need to be right, the need to feel safe, and the need to be liked.[9] Let's explore each in further detail.

THE DESIRE FOR CONTROL

The first core craving is the desire for control. This desire is difficult to confront because it seems to help us in all walks of life. At work, we want people to be organized, logical, and capable of operating with a degree of stability. We don't like it when folks are flailing around in an out-of-control or inconsistent manner. Businesses and the people who work in them are expected to operate with precision and poise, and we put a high price tag on those who are in control.

At home, control is also highly valued. We find comfort in depending on our loved ones. We want them to provide us with stability, and we expect them to behave in a controlled and consistent manner. When our home and our family are under control, it brings a sense of relief and reward. We appreciate it when our loved ones are organized and dedicated to a plan or a set of operating procedures.

We love it when the dishes are clean, clothes are folded, and the pantry is stocked with our favorite goodies.

Control gives us a sense of safety and security when everything goes according to plan. But when things turn toward chaos, when someone in the family is out of control, or when someone at work intentionally breaks the rules, we can feel frustrated and downright angry. We want everything to be under control so badly because we feel ill-equipped to deal with the chaos.

But chaos and change are the new normal, and stability is a false hope. We can no longer rely on control. No matter how firmly we try to grasp it, control as a strategy is ill-equipped for the modern world. It doesn't actually help us reach our goals, and in fact, it can hold us back from achieving them. If we over-rely on controlling behaviors, we can get stuck in a downward spiral that restricts and constrains our energy and enthusiasm, and limits our ability to thrive in the modern world.

The table below provides a few controlling behaviors we should eliminate and a few behaviors we should replace them with.

NEGATIVE BEHAVIORS	POSITIVE BEHAVIORS
Micromanaging	Trusting
Excessive monitoring	Checking in periodically
Dismissing feelings or emotions	Acknowledging and accepting emotions
Making decisions for others	Involving others in decision-making
Withholding information	Sharing important information

THE NEED TO BE RIGHT

Human beings have a deep-rooted need to be right. From an early age, we are taught that knowing is valuable, and we are rewarded for having the right answers. As time goes on, being right becomes a habit, and anything less starts to sting. Eventually, this need shifts into overdrive and becomes a distracting desire that blurs the lines between seeking truth and feeding the ego.

We've all watched this play out at work; perhaps in a discussion with the goal of solving a problem. You propose an idea that you're proud of, and then a colleague suggests an alternative. Both proposals are good, but both of you dig in your heels and start debating. Before you know it, you are arguing over meaningless details, trying to convince each other that your idea is right and the other's idea is wrong. The discussion turns to an argument, and you find yourself frustrated and at odds with your colleague, and most of the people in the room.

This can also happen at home. While eating dinner, your teenage daughter points out that you misstated a fact that you were certain you had right. All of a sudden, that nice family meal and conversation turns into a heated argument where your daughter ends up crying, and you feel like a jerk. Apologies no longer matter because you pushed it too far. Your desire to be right just damaged the relationship.

The need to be right is a distracting desire that everyone pursues at one point or another. It is a hallmark of the ego, and one of those repetitive patterns that few ever recognize they're caught in. But if you can see it for what it is—a distracting desire that produces little to no value—you can free yourself from it. Noticing your need to be right can help you shift your attention to more important things.

So next time you feel the need to be right, pay close attention to your behaviors. Watch out for the negative behaviors in the following table, and shift toward positive behaviors. Consciously tell yourself that you will let go of this distracting desire and move forward with a more open and collaborative mindset.

NEGATIVE BEHAVIORS	POSITIVE BEHAVIORS
Arguing to prove a point	Asking for other opinions
Dismissing others' ideas without consideration	Acknowledging and accepting others' ideas
Interrupting others to correct them	Listening and asking clarifying questions
Assuming you know what is best	Assuming you are missing something
Refusing to admit you are wrong	Admitting when you are wrong

THE NEED TO BE SAFE

We live in a world that seems dangerous. There are threats all around; if we aren't careful, something might jump out and bite us. This mindset is the primary driver of the need to be safe. From an early age, we are taught to care for ourselves and stay out of harm's way. Our parents, hopefully, taught us not to touch a hot stove or stand too close to the fire because they didn't want us to get burned. Our teachers taught us to read, do math, and think scientifically so we could learn about the world and avoid the harm it can do. Our employers taught us to follow processes and procedures because they didn't want us to mess things up and fail to deliver the products or services we were committed to delivering. The list goes on and on, but the point is clear. Safety is a priority, and we all have an innate desire to be safe.

Instilling a need to be safe is wise but has a downside. The downside is that it holds us back. It makes us play small and avoid the risks needed in a complicated and ever-changing world. Playing small turns into lower performance and dissatisfaction. Before you know it, you are like a wallflower at a middle school dance, standing alone in the corner while everyone else is dancing and having a great time.

This can all be avoided if we realize that safety doesn't come from comfort. As humans, we often miss this point because we confuse comfort with security. We think if we just stick to what we know, we'll be safe. But comfort zones are tricky. They feel like warm blankets, but they can suffocate growth if we wrap ourselves up in them. The reality is that safety comes from resilience, from building the skills and mindset to navigate uncertainty, not hide from it. Resilience is our safety net, reassuring us that we can handle whatever the world throws at us. The world isn't static, and neither are we. When we step out of that metaphorical corner, take a deep breath, and join the dance—even if we stumble a bit—we discover that's where the real growth happens. That's where fun and fulfillment lives.

Finding balance in our need for safety is crucial. We need to maintain a desire to protect ourselves, and recognize when it starts to limit us. This recognition is a powerful capability that we should all try to develop. To help you, I recommend paying attention to a few key behaviors related to this need to feel safe. Like the other distracting desires, the need to feel safe is expressed in both positive and negative ways. The following table highlights five positive and five negative behaviors that stem from this desire to feel safe.

NEGATIVE BEHAVIORS	POSITIVE BEHAVIORS
Avoiding conflict	Engaging in respectful disagreements
Defensiveness	Open to feedback
Analysis paralysis	Making informed decisions
Risk aversion	Involving others in decision-making
Withdrawing	Engaging with composure

THE NEED TO BE LIKED

One thing I've come to understand about people is that we all share a common need to be liked. This is a universal truth, even for those who are rugged individualists, appear standoffish, or dislike people in general. The desire to be liked is a fundamental part of our human nature, deeply ingrained in our DNA.

As social creatures, we need to be liked, as it helps us survive and thrive. We want others to see us, understand us, and value us. We want to be part of a community bigger than ourselves, and we know that being around others will help us achieve our goals. We also want positive recognition and validation to show that others respect or admire us; we shouldn't feel bad about that. But when this need goes unchecked, it shifts from a natural desire to a compulsive force, pulling us away from who we truly are and into a performance designed for approval rather than connection.

Whenever I think about the need to be liked, I recall a former colleague. I'll call her Clara to maintain her privacy because the story isn't flattering.

Clara was a driven and successful professional who was liked by a few but annoying to many. You've probably met people like her. She was agreeable and willing to help but also incredibly needy. She constantly sought recognition and validation and wanted others to understand how valuable she was. She had a persistent, almost anxious presence—always nearby, always watching, as if waiting for a signal that she was appreciated. Clara hovered because she wanted to be recognized, validated, and approved. Her need to be liked was on overdrive.

Now, Clara wasn't entirely at fault. She was a lovely person with a kind heart and a strong desire to succeed. She was also very smart and capable of doing the work she was hired to do. But over time, her incessant behaviors—driven by her desire to be liked—started to annoy people and pull their attention away from her contributions. Instead of focusing on her work, they could only see their negative experiences while working with her. They started talking about her behind her back and criticizing her character. The straw broke the camel's back when they avoided her and excluded her from conversations and meetings. Clara realized what was happening when it was too late and lost it. She was fired for a lack of performance and being difficult to work with.

Clara's story is familiar to those consumed with the need to be liked. It reminds us that this need can be harmful if we don't know how to manage it. The desire to be liked is only distracting when it's in overdrive. In moderation, it can be constructive. But when it takes over, it can become destructive and lead to several negative behaviors. The following table outlines a few of these behaviors and highlights five positive actions that emerge from a more balanced version of this desire.

NEGATIVE BEHAVIORS	POSITIVE BEHAVIORS
People-pleasing	Connecting with people
Seeking recognition and validation	Monitoring your own performance
Disrespecting boundaries	Encouraging inclusivity
Avoiding conflict	Being approachable and supportive
Inconsistent decision-making	Seeking consensus

Clearing the path

In this chapter, we examined how powerful and distracting our desires can be. Just as Anakin Skywalker was led astray by his unchecked cravings, we, too, can be distracted by desires that promise much but deliver little. These desires, whether for material success, approval, or control, can steer us off course, pulling us away from what truly matters.

The key to eliminating distracting desires lies in developing discernment. We must learn to distinguish between desires that align with our deepest values and those that only serve to clutter our minds and hearts. By recognizing and eliminating these distracting desires, we can reduce the cognitive load that weighs us down, allowing us to focus our limited energy and attention on pursuits that genuinely fulfill us. The process is challenging, but the rewards are profound: greater clarity, improved decision-making, and a life lived in alignment with our true purpose.

As you continue into the next chapter, remember that each decision to discard a distracting desire is a step toward a more focused and fulfilling life. It's about peeling back the layers of wants that cloud your vision and finding the ones that align with who you are.

So, the next time a desire beckons, ask yourself: Is this leading me closer to my true path, or is it a distraction I must let go of? This subtle shift helps you clear the path ahead and confidently move toward your goals.

Chapter Summary

- We must discard distracting desires if we want to shift our attention. We cannot have it all.
- Many of our desires are fleeting, superficial, or misaligned with our deeper values and long-term goals.
- Distracting desires can lead us away from our authentic selves and hinder our long-term success. Although tempting, they often steer us in the wrong direction.
- We must develop discernment to identify and discard these distracting desires. We must learn to differentiate between fleeting distractions and desires that align with our deepest values and long-term vision.
- Eliminating unnecessary desires reduces cognitive load, leading to clearer thinking, better decision-making, and a more focused, fulfilling life.
- The ego drives four core cravings: the desire for control, the need to be right, the need to feel safe, and the need to be liked.
- Knowing what desires come from the ego can help us shift our attention.

THREE

Elevate: Focus on What Matters Most

"The main thing is to keep the main thing the main thing."
~ Stephen R. Covey

Many years ago, I experienced one of the most chaotic weeks of my professional life. The chaos was self-inflicted, directly resulting from not paying attention to my attention. As a leader, my role required me to oversee various tasks, but that week, I found myself stuck in the minutiae of every project. At the time, I thought I was overworked and overwhelmed, but looking back, I realize that wasn't the case.

It was a week like many others where I was buried in the details of multiple projects. I reviewed financial reports for one team, brainstormed marketing strategies with another, and mediated interpersonal issues in a third. I had a keynote speech scheduled for an upcoming leadership conference and several email messages to get through. It wasn't just the volume of tasks that was overwhelming; it was the level of detail each task required. I had delegated a ton to my team but was still caught in the weeds, losing sight of the bigger picture.

I felt exhausted and overwhelmed, but it was entirely my own doing. My attention was scattered across too many things, and then, one day, I hit a tipping point. A colleague from another division popped into my office to ask me a question, and I lost it. Feeling overwhelmed and frustrated with the interruption, I lost my cool. I didn't actually scream and completely fly off the handle, but I was rude and critical and gave her a piece of my mind. It wasn't my best moment.

Later that day, my boss called me to discuss what happened. He wanted to hear my side of the story but wasn't pleased. He told me my behavior was out of line for someone in my position and asked me what the heck I was thinking. He reminded me that leaders in our organization were expected to treat others with respect and to work with people, not just through them. And he clarified that an incident like this couldn't happen again. I went home that day with my tail between my legs.

It was a jarring wake-up call. Later that night, I talked to my wife and completely broke down. I knew I was wrong and felt terrible about it. I was burning the candle at both ends and pushing myself too hard. My bad behavior was one thing, but the real problem was my unrealistic expectations about how I could manage my workload and attention.

In my quest to be the perfect leader, I had lost sight of an essential point about leadership.

Leadership
is about how
we show up.

Leadership is about more than what we do. Leadership is about how we show up. It is about more than mere accomplishments, the tasks we complete, and the quality of our work. Leadership is an elevated endeavor that requires us to operate at a higher level to provide support and guidance to those we lead. In other words, it's an endeavor that requires an elevated level of consciousness.

Lessons learned

Whenever I look back on that incident, I feel incredibly embarrassed. I treated my colleague poorly, and I acted like a jerk. I apologized to her the next day, but the damage was done. I lost focus on my primary leadership role by pulling myself into the depths of too many tasks. It was a harsh but much-needed wake-up call that taught me several lessons about maintaining an elevated perspective.

Leaders aren't supposed to work themselves into overwhelm. Our role demands that we keep our attention elevated, focus on the bigger picture, set priorities, problem-solve, and help others do the same. Ultimately, we don't get credit for dotting all the i's and crossing all the t's. We get credit for inspiring and supporting people and helping them achieve something they never thought possible.

Leaders are only effective when they work with and through others.

Prioritizing results over relationships is a flawed strategy because the leader's primary role is to inspire and support others. This realization dawned on me as I reflected on the incident. I sent an incredibly damaging message by prioritizing what was on my plate and deprioritizing my relationship with my colleague. I was not a leader worth following. Instead of prioritizing my own productivity, task completion, and goal achievement, I should have prioritized how I could help my colleague with hers.

The poet and author Maya Angelou wrote, "People will forget what you said, people will forget what you did, but people will never forget how you made them feel." When I lost my cool, I acted foolishly, leaving someone feeling unappreciated and undervalued. With my cutting words, I hurt someone who didn't deserve it—someone who was just trying to do her job.

Leadership is about creating and nurturing relationships that inspire, motivate, and endure challenges. When the focus shifts too heavily towards results, at the expense of the people achieving those results, teamwork breaks down. Trust, loyalty, and mutual respect can quickly erode when we ignore or discount our relationships.

State matters

When it comes to leadership, our state matters more than our substance. In my relentless pursuit of perfection, I focused almost exclusively on the tangible outcomes of my work—the reports, the strategies, the speeches—believing that these were the ultimate measures of my success as a leader. However, this focus on substance overshadowed the emotional and mental state from which I operated. A friend helped me realize that how I showed up—the energy I brought, my attitude, my overall presence—had a bigger impact on people than I'd ever considered. It was a fundamental shift in my understanding of leadership. I started to see that a leader's state of mind—how aware, grounded, and steady they are—sets the tone for everyone else. A positive, calm presence isn't just about good vibes; it shapes how people work together, trust each other, and develop new ideas. In other words, *who* you are matters as much, if not more, than *what* you do.

This was a wake-up call to take my own mental and emotional health seriously, to keep myself grounded, knowing that it made me more resilient and sharper as a leader.

For a long time, I ran on fumes. I tried to be everywhere, take on every project, and hit every goal, losing touch with any sense of balance or purpose. I pushed so hard that I started to operate on autopilot, going through the motions without real focus or care. It chipped away at my ability to make sound decisions, drained my empathy, and made me oblivious to the needs of the people around me. I wasn't fully present anywhere.

This state hurt the quality of my decisions, interactions, and, ultimately, my ability to connect. It drove home the importance of self-awareness and balancing my workload—not just for my own sanity but because it's essential for the organization. I realized that real strength isn't about piling on more and more but knowing when to pause, step back, and protect my energy. It's in that space that we lead with real presence.

The power of conscious leadership

The incident with my colleague taught me that my attention wasn't in the right place. I didn't get it immediately then, but as the years passed and my experiences grew, I came to appreciate a concept known as conscious leadership.[1]

Conscious leadership emphasizes self-awareness, mindfulness, and the ability to lead with empathy and authenticity. At its core, conscious leadership is about leading from a place of awareness and choice rather than reacting unconsciously to situations and people.

This idea marked a pivotal shift in my approach to leadership and, ultimately, my approach to life. Being conscious isn't just about making informed decisions or being aware of your surroundings; it's about being deeply connected with your inner state, values, and the impact you have on others. It's about being conscious of what's happening in you, others, and the world.

It took years for these learnings to sink in, but they helped me grow and become a more conscious leader over time. By pursuing a higher level of consciousness, I learned to lead with my mind and heart, fostering an environment where empathy, understanding, and genuine connections flourished. It became evident that consciousness was required to inspire and uplift others, transform challenges into growth opportunities, and lead by example. It turns out that consciousness is a prerequisite for subtle shifts.

Taking the higher ground

Do you ever feel like you are operating unconsciously? Do you ever feel stuck in the weeds, struggling to keep up with the endless tasks and challenges that life throws your way? Life and leadership can feel like a battle where we fight like hell to complete our work while simultaneously building barriers to defend our position. Sometimes, we operate on autopilot, completely unaware of what we are doing or our effect on others.

What can we do to turn off the autopilot? Productivity gurus tell us to write things down and to capture all our commitments. They tell us to prioritize, streamline, and optimize our workflows. They offer tools and techniques to help us manage our tasks more efficiently. Unfortunately, much of this advice doesn't work because it buries us in content.

Instead of elevating our attention and focusing on context, productivity advice drives our attention down to content. Do you remember the questions I asked in Chapter One? Unless we notice that our attention is anchored in content and realize we need to shift it to context, we will find ourselves overwhelmed and fighting an uphill battle that keeps getting harder.

The Chinese military strategist Sun Tzu once said, "He who occupies the high ground...will fight to advantage."[2] This principle, articulated over two thousand years ago, underscores the tactical and psychological benefits of holding superior terrain in conflict. Tzu's wisdom, distilled through the ages, echoes in the annals of history and modern warfare. It is equally significant in elevating our attention and personal effectiveness. If you can mentally take the high ground, shifting your attention away from content toward context, you will have a significant advantage in all you encounter.

From the ancient scrolls of Sun Tzu to the fields of Gettysburg, the importance of high ground comes sharply into focus. The Battle of Gettysburg was a pivotal moment in the American Civil War, and it exemplifies Sun Tzu's teachings.

Upon arriving at Gettysburg, Union Brigadier General John Buford immediately recognized the tactical significance of the elevated terrain south of the town.[3] His decision to hold this ground until reinforcements could arrive was instrumental in the Union's eventual victory. The Confederate forces, led by General Robert E. Lee, found themselves repeatedly thwarted by the Union's advantageous position, culminating in the failed assault known as "Pickett's Charge". The Union's control of Cemetery Ridge provided superior vantage points and a morale boost. John Buford's critical decision to take the higher ground shows the power of Sun Tzu's strategy—fighting from an elevated position is a competitive advantage.

In the modern era, the battle for high ground has ascended from the terrestrial to the celestial. Satellites now orbit the Earth and play a crucial role in contemporary conflicts. Just before I sat down to write this chapter, CNN reported that Russia is increasingly frustrated with the West's satellite infrastructure.[4] They are looking into ways to destroy that infrastructure with a nuclear-powered weapon because their war with Ukraine, which many believed would last days, is now dragging on for years. It turns out the Russians aren't so happy with Ukraine's ability to monitor troop movements and maneuvers from an elevated perspective. This real-time intelligence gathered from space proves to be a significant disadvantage for Russia.

The metaphor of holding the higher ground extends beyond the battlefield into the boardroom and daily life. In business, as in war, seeking a higher vantage point is metaphorically valid. Leaders and entrepreneurs often find themselves bogged down by the day-to-day and the here-and-now. This myopic and reactive perspective can limit what a leader notices. It keeps them from seeing strategic opportunities and threats. Just as generals must survey the battlefield from an elevated position to make informed decisions, leaders must elevate their perspective to be effective. This same principle applies to all of us. By rising above the fray, we can identify trends, opportunities, and challenges that remain unseen from the ground level.

Elevating our perspective and capitalizing on the strategic advantage involves more than just a physical change. It requires a mental shift in how we look at the many things that compete for our attention. It requires continually learning and adapting to see the forest for the trees, recognize patterns, and anticipate moves before they are made. It requires us to zoom out.

Zooming out

In 2020, the coronavirus pandemic swept across the globe. The virus killed millions of people, but it also played a cruel game with our attention. It caught us by surprise and shifted our attention in unexpected ways. The sudden constraints of quarantine pushed many into the thicket of daily worries. For others, the lockdown was a chance to finally relax, reevaluate, and spend quality time with their loved ones. A few even picked up entirely new hobbies—like baking bread or learning guitar—filling the silence with something meaningful.

The toll on our ability to connect was profound and far-reaching. For many of us, it was a disruption that completely changed our perspective on so many fronts. That may be why Zoom's video conferencing platform became an unlikely hero of the pandemic narrative.

As the world locked down, Zoom emerged as a lifeline, bridging the gap that social distancing created. It allowed us to maintain a semblance of normalcy and created what many started to call the new normal. Some people loved it, while others hated it, but there's no denying that Zoom provided a sense of connection and routine in a time of uncertainty, growing quickly as a result. In December 2019, Zoom catered to 10 million daily users, but by April 2020—just four months later—that number jumped to 300 million.[5] The pandemic fueled the Zoom fire. It shifted attention toward technologies that could save us from our isolation.

Amidst the digital fanfare surrounding Zoom, another innovation, also named Zoom, captured my household's attention.

Istvan Banyai's *Zoom* is a wordless children's book published in 1995, which became a source of joy and wonder for my child and me.[6] It did so because while Zoom, the technology platform, let us back into our school and work lives, *Zoom*, the book, taught us how important it is to zoom out.

Banyai's book is hard to explain in words, so I encourage you to check it out. Here's the gist. The book begins with nothing but a picture of a rooster's head. At first, you can't tell what you are looking at, but more is revealed as you turn the pages. On page four, you think you are looking at two people looking through a window at a rooster. On page seven, you realize that the rooster and people are just toys because you see a child playing with them in a farm playscape. By page nine, you realize the child and playscape are a magazine cover, and by page twelve, you realize that the magazine is being held by a woman on a cruise ship. The perspective shifts continue as you flip through the pages, zoom out, and take on a different perspective.

Zoom is not just a book; it's an experience. Lauded by *The New York Times* and *Publishers Weekly* as a fantastic children's book and a "stunning experience", it poignantly reminds us of the importance of questioning and altering our viewpoints.[7,8] It beautifully illustrates the value of elevating our attention and reminds us that what we see in front of us is only a fraction of reality.

The first time I went through this book, a sudden and profound insight struck me: our perspective really matters, and elevating attention is an excellent way to shift our perspective. As I watched each page reveal a broader context than the last, I realized that too

Elevating attention is an excellent way to shift our perspective.

much focus can keep us from being effective. This is important because it flies in the face of conventional wisdom on success and productivity. Most people tell us that our struggles are due to a lack of focus, not too much of it.

Often, when faced with an opportunity or challenge, we zoom in. We dig into the details and focus on small things that rarely provide us with what we need. Think of the last time you faced a pressing deadline or a complex problem. Your instinctive reaction might have been to hunker down, narrow your focus, and pore over every minute detail. But this desire could be a distraction. If we zoom in too much, we will miss the forest for the trees.

Elevated aspirations

The incident with my colleague taught me to be careful about what I pursue. Some of our goals are true aspirations, while others are merely distractions. True aspirations are those that align with a deeper set of values and drive us towards achievements that are meaningful to many. They aren't S.M.A.R.T. goals. They are more significant than that.

In the last chapter, I discussed the importance of discarding distracting desires. Some desires can capture our attention, lead us away from our core path, and pull us into a pit of despair. Often disguised as attractive opportunities, they ultimately lead us down the wrong path. They are like mirages in a desert, promising refreshment and relief that vanish upon closer inspection.

In this chapter, I want to show you the opposite of these distracting desires. I want you to think about how you shift your attention toward elevated aspirations. These are the higher goals that align with our authentic selves. They come from deep within and align nicely with things we all strive for, like our mission, vision, purpose, and core values. They have a way of pushing us toward the best version of ourselves, and they also have a way of bringing out the best in others. The four elevated aspirations are the desire to inspire, the need to understand, the call to connect, and the craving to contribute.

THE DESIRE TO INSPIRE

The desire to inspire is the opposite of the need for control that I referenced in the last chapter. Shifting your focus from control to inspiration may feel subtle, but it's transformative. It leads to higher performance and lasting success for you and those around you. People don't want to be controlled or manipulated. They want to be inspired because inspiration is a much more powerful force.

Inspiration doesn't come from managing every detail or dictating how things should unfold. It comes from stepping back, letting go of control, and giving others the room to grow. It's about showing what's possible, not forcing a specific outcome. While control may give you a quick sense of security, inspiration creates a ripple effect far beyond your immediate influence. When you lead by example instead of through micromanagement or rigidity, you allow others to rise to their potential—on their terms.

Control is narrow, driven by the fear that things will spiral into chaos if you loosen your grip. But inspiration is expansive. It's rooted in freedom, creativity, and trust. When you focus on control, you often protect your comfort zone and ego. When you focus on inspiration, you invest in the growth and potential of others, trusting them to find their own path to success. And here's the thing: people will surprise you when you give them that space.

Now, you might be thinking, *"But I'm not the inspirational type."* Maybe you don't see yourself as someone who naturally motivates others, or perhaps you've never aspired to be the kind of person who inspires a room full of people. But the truth is, this ability lies within all of us. It may be dormant, but it's there. It often waits for the right moment or mindset shift to spring to life.

You don't need a formal leadership role to inspire others, and you don't need a title or a spotlight. Inspiration comes from how you live, show up, and empower those around you to think bigger and do better. The desire to inspire lives within you, and you can tap into it simply by shifting your attention, letting go of control, and recognizing that this capability is yours to unleash. Here are a few questions to ask and ideas to investigate if you want to unlock this elevated aspiration.

What do I find inspiring?

If you want to inspire, you need to be inspired. Thinking about what inspires you can help you identify the assumptions and actions that inspire others.

What do I want to inspire others to do?

If you want to inspire others, you must be clear about what you are leading them to. Without a target to aim at, it will be hard to be clear and compelling.

When was the last time I felt inspired by someone? What did they do?

We can learn a lot from our own experiences. Take time to reflect on what you found inspiring and look at what others did to inspire you.

When was the last time I inspired someone? How did I do that?

Remember, you can learn a lot from your past actions. I am confident that you have inspired others at some point. How did you do that?

How can I create space for others to shine without my direct oversight?

We don't inspire people by telling them what to do. We inspire people by making requests, offering suggestions, modeling the way, and giving them space. We can't control their every move.

In what areas of my life am I holding on too tightly, and what might happen if I let go?

We must let go of our controlling tendencies before we can hope to inspire others. We will fail to inspire others if we keep falling back on bad habits.

THE NEED TO UNDERSTAND

In the last chapter, we discussed how damaging it can be to have an incessant need to be right. Demanding that we are right damages relationships and prevents us from performing at our peak. That is why, in this chapter, I'm providing an alternative. What if instead of always trying to be right, we focused our attention on trying to understand? That is what this subtle shift is about.

The need to understand is an elevated aspiration worth pursuing. It results in greater teamwork, collaboration, satisfaction, and innovation. When we go out into the world with a high degree of curiosity and open-mindedness, we build stronger connections and find new ways to solve old problems. We also experience perspective shifts that can radically transform our lives and our experiences.

Several years ago, I worked with a client who struggled with always needing to be right. He was a bright and relatively competent business owner, and for much of his career, he was rewarded for his knowledge. But as his business grew, new and unanticipated challenges did, too. Everything became much more complicated and complex, and he struggled to adapt because he wasn't curious and open.

One day, he told me he was tired and frustrated. Everyone around him kept questioning his decisions, and he was sick of it. He lost his temper and blurted out a few things he didn't mean to say. The problem was that his employees were no longer willing to tolerate it. He lost three top performers in key leadership positions in a span of six months. As they exited, they told me they were leaving because they could no longer accept his arrogance.

The turmoil around the resignations led my client to an epiphany. He recognized that his need to be right was a major problem and decided to make a change. Luckily for him, the change was only a subtle shift away. Everything changed once he shifted his attention from being right to understanding. People began to be honest with him and shared their opinions. They took on more responsibility and started to hold themselves accountable. But all of that paled alongside how he felt about himself. Within one year of the subtle shift in attention, he started to enjoy work more, relaxed with his family, and felt more confident in his team.

This is just one example of the power of subtle shifts. When we shift our attention away from being right and toward understanding, we completely change the dynamics in our psyche and relationships.

As in the previous section, here are a few questions you can ask if you want to dig deeper into this elevated aspiration.

What can I be more curious about?

It is hard to be stubborn and curious simultaneously, but this simple question can plant curiosity seeds that grow over time. Ask it often, and you will replace your need to be right.

What clarifying questions can I ask before responding with my own opinion?

When you are in the heat of a conversation or debate, you might be quick to respond or cut people off. Instead, ask clarifying questions to see if you can understand more about what the other person is saying.

In what situations do I feel most defensive, and how can I shift toward curiosity instead?

We usually have triggers that put us into a defensive state. Identifying these can help us choose different responses when these triggers undoubtedly arise.

How might understanding someone else's perspective change the way I approach challenges?

Other perspectives are worth knowing, particularly when we accept that there are many versions of "right". By asking this question, you allow others to have a voice and show that you are a team player.

What questions can I ask to expand my understanding?

Asking big, bold, open-ended questions is the biggest step to increasing your understanding. Great rewards lie on the other side of open-ended questions.

THE CALL TO CONNECT

We want to connect but don't always have the necessary skills. We think it's about exchanging pleasantries or pushing buttons on a social media platform when it's really something completely different.

At its core, connection is about integrating different perspectives and experiences into a stronger whole than the individual pieces. It's about discovering common ground and complementary capabilities. It isn't just a "nice to have". Connection is essential for doing our best work and living fully.

But here's the challenge: our instinct is to pull away and protect ourselves when life gets tough. This urge to retreat makes connection harder when we need it most. Instead of building bridges, we isolate ourselves, which only leads to further isolation. We need to put in the effort to break the cycle, and when we do so, the benefits are huge.

Connection makes us stronger—emotionally, mentally, and practically. Teams that connect and trust each other solve problems faster and more creatively than those that don't. At home, strong connections build better relationships and emotionally healthy families. In other areas of life, the synergy created when people connect can lead to results none of us could accomplish alone.

Let me share a quick story. Several years ago, I worked with a leadership team that didn't work very well together. They were incredibly disconnected because they didn't like each other and preferred to focus on their responsibilities. Each person focused on their goals and avoided the others like the plague. Tension built up and leaked out into the organization in a very damaging way. They started losing business because they weren't coordinating or cooperating. Then, one day, after a pretty big fallout, they discovered a subtle shift.

The shift was simple. The team had to stop focusing on self-preservation and start focusing on team success. To the outside observer, this was a significant shift, but, in truth, it came about slowly.

One day, I was having a conversation with three of the team members, when they realized that their attention was in the wrong place. Instead of paying attention to what they needed from others, they needed to pay attention to what others needed from them; instead of focusing on their division goals, they needed to focus on company goals.

Then came the epiphany. Instead of working in isolation, they needed more collaboration, cooperation, and coordination, and none of this would happen without connection. As the conversation unfolded, their lack of connection became more evident, and they saw the error in their ways. They had been working in stovepipes and were finally tired of it.

At that moment, they committed to connecting more often and asked me to facilitate several meetings to help them along. The results were remarkable. The more they connected, the more they began to trust one another. Conversations that once felt like battles turned into discussions where they worked toward mutually beneficial solutions. They shifted their attention from self-preservation to team success—not because they had to, but because they realized the team's success ultimately benefited them all.

This team demonstrated the power of subtle shifts in attention and taught me how important it was to direct attention toward connection and away from isolation. Here are a few of the questions and ideas I shared with them to help them make this shift.

Am I connected or isolated?

Take a moment to reflect on whether you're actively engaging with others or keeping a distance. True connection happens when we choose to reach out, even if it feels uncomfortable.

What am I trying to do on my own, but shouldn't?

Consider areas where collaboration could ease the load. Often, we take on too much ourselves, missing opportunities to harness the strengths of those around us.

What can I do to connect, collaborate, cooperate, and coordinate?

Think about simple actions that could strengthen your teamwork, like regular check-ins or sharing resources. Effective connection requires conscious, small steps toward shared goals.

How can I use the strengths of the people around me?

Everyone brings something unique to the table, so look for ways to leverage these strengths for better outcomes. When we recognize and utilize each other's skills, the whole team grows stronger.

What can I do to strengthen my relationships?

Investing time and effort into understanding and supporting others builds trust. Strong relationships are built on empathy, respect, and consistent connection.

THE CRAVING TO CONTRIBUTE

When you think about your work, where do you put most of your attention? Do you want other people to like you or do you want to simply contribute? Remember Clara from the last chapter? She desperately wanted to be liked, suppressed her craving to contribute, and failed to stand out. Clara lost her job because she worried more about being charming than contributing. She put her ego ahead of execution and prioritized appearance over outcomes.

The craving to contribute is a natural desire in each of us. Whenever I think of this elevated aspiration, I think about how everyone feels in the initial weeks of a new job. Remember when you started your latest job? I'll bet you were a bit nervous but filled with excitement, anticipation, and a strong desire to contribute. You likely had a vision of all you hoped to accomplish and hoped others would appreciate you for all you brought to the table. No one starts a new job with a desire to coast or do nothing.

Yet, over time, something shifts. That initial craving to contribute can fade as routines settle in and the desire to be accepted grows louder. We all want a sense of belonging, but when that longing turns into a need for constant approval, it starts holding us back. Clara's story reminds us how this desire can become a distraction, drawing our attention away from meaningful work and toward pleasing others. It is a subtle shift in the opposite direction and one we want to avoid.

To connect to your craving to contribute, turn your focus to the impact you want to make. Instead of thinking, "Will they like this?" try asking, "How will this move us forward?" This change in perspective might feel small, but it is just the shift we need to make progress. If Clara had looked for opportunities to contribute, she could have turned herself into someone who put service above self, which is precisely what our organizations need.

When we embrace this craving, we create momentum and end up doing things that matter. Our ideas and efforts start to carry more weight, and we become people others look to for guidance. If you

Turn your focus
to the impact you
want to make.

want to lean into this elevated aspiration, ask yourself the following questions and reflect on how you can contribute.

How can I make a solid contribution?

Think about where your skills and strengths align with the needs of others. By focusing on areas where you can make the most impact, you can contribute to the team's success and growth.

What can I do without approval?

Identify tasks or initiatives where you can take the lead without waiting for permission. Acting autonomously shows confidence in your role and demonstrates your commitment to adding value.

How can I shift my focus from "fitting in" to "standing out"?

Instead of aiming to blend in, look for ways to make a memorable impact through your unique approach or perspective. Standing out is about offering value others may not see. It creates a positive ripple effect in an organization.

What small steps can I take to contribute?

Contributions don't always have to be grand. Small, consistent actions build credibility over time. Whether offering support on a project or sharing ideas in a meeting, each step reinforces your commitment.

What is the unique contribution that only I can make?

Reflect on your specific skills, experiences, or insights that are uniquely yours. Once you identify your unique strengths, you can find ways to bring value in ways no one else can.

Elevate your attention

This chapter explored the importance of focusing on what matters most. As leaders, our attention is often pulled in countless directions, but effective leadership requires us to rise above the chaos and maintain an elevated perspective. The story I shared about my failure to do so was a harsh reminder that leadership is not just about getting things done—it's about how we show up, prioritize, and make those subtle shifts in our attention that align us with what truly matters.

The lesson here is clear: when we allow ourselves to get bogged down in the minutiae, we lose sight of the bigger picture. By making small, deliberate shifts in how we focus our attention, we can zoom out, elevate our consciousness, and ensure that our actions align with our most important goals and values. These subtle adjustments improve our effectiveness and have a ripple effect on our relationships and overall well-being.

As we move into Part Two of this book, remember that attention drives everything. It is a limited resource that declines throughout the day, so be conscious of how you use it. By elevating your attention, you will be better equipped to shift your assumptions, which is an equally challenging endeavor.

Chapter Summary

- When we're caught in the weeds, we lose sight of what matters most. If we want to shift our attention, we must elevate our perspective.
- Leadership is about more than what we do. It's about how we show up.
- Prioritizing relationships over tasks isn't just good practice; it's essential. Leaders who inspire and support others build stronger, more resilient teams.
- Overextending ourselves leads to burnout and diminished effectiveness. Recognizing our limits and knowing when to step back is vital to maintaining a clear mind and a healthy leadership presence.
- Conscious leadership is about leading with awareness, empathy, and authenticity. By staying connected to our values and understanding our impact on others, we can lead in a way that makes a difference.
- Shifting our attention from content to context gives us the higher ground. By zooming out and gaining a broader perspective, we can navigate challenges more effectively and seize opportunities others might miss.
- Elevated aspirations align with our deepest values and lead to sustainable success. These goals demand more of us but offer far greater rewards, leading to growth, fulfillment, and a meaningful impact on others.

PART 2

Shifting Assumptions

FOUR

Contemplate: Think About Your Thinking

"Muddy water, let stand, becomes clear."

~ Lao Tzu

At a pivotal moment in World War II, when despair loomed large, the direction of the free world rested on the shoulders of a few key figures. Prominent among them was Winston Churchill, a name now synonymous with resilient leadership and strategic mastery. Yet, Churchill's approach to navigating this monumental crisis was anything but conventional.

In 1941, as Britain confronted its gravest challenge, with Europe overwhelmed by the Nazi regime, Churchill's leadership style emerged as a paradox. While his powerful speeches and unwavering spirit rallied a nation, his unique morning routine set him apart from traditional images of dynamic leadership.[1]

Churchill's day would often begin not in the flurry of urgent meetings or at the helm of command centers but in the quiet of his bedroom. There, in the comfort of his bed, accompanied by a full English breakfast, cigars, and scotch, he engaged in deep contemplation. Far from a display of laziness, these hours were spent meticulously analyzing the complex dynamics of the war. He examined domestic and international affairs, dissected military strategies, and pondered over the morale of a nation under siege.

This practice of morning reflection, unconventional as it may seem, was instrumental in crafting the subtle yet profound shifts in strategy that would eventually lead Britain from a state of vulnerability to one of formidable strength. Through these reflective sessions, Churchill was able to envision and enact strategies that steered the country through its darkest hours and inspired the Allied victory.

Churchill's routine prompts us to reconsider our preconceptions of effective leadership. How does one reconcile the image of a leader, often envisioned as perpetually active and decisively on the move, with that of Churchill, who spent critical morning hours in his bed? How did such an unorthodox approach—one that looked to others like laziness—contribute to his legendary status in leading a nation during wartime? The answer is simple. Churchill made time to think.

By making time to think, Churchill demonstrated that effective leadership is not about constant action; it's also about thoughtful deliberation. His ability to carve out these periods of reflection amidst the chaos of war allowed him to process information, consider various perspectives, and make strategic and impactful decisions. It also allowed him to identify subtle shifts that others would have missed.

Churchill was a master of nuance and understood the power of subtle shifts. Look no further than his rhetorical skill, strategic ambiguity, and diplomatic finesse to see this in action. He crafted speeches that resonated with the emotional state of his audience, utilized ambiguity to maintain strategic flexibility, and navigated complex diplomatic waters with a keen understanding of human psychology. Churchill's ability to adapt his strategies in response to changing circumstances, coupled with his deep emotional insight, allowed him to connect with people and lead effectively. However, this intricate blend of leadership qualities would have been impossible without the deliberate time he set aside for contemplation.

Making time to think

In today's world, where information hits us from every angle, contemplation has become increasingly rare. The constant flow of social and traditional media updates puts us in a constant state of consumption. We rarely pause to digest or reflect, but that is precisely what we need to do. Profound insights and solutions to our complex problems emerge in the moments of reflection and contemplation. It is in these moments that we discover the most significant subtle shifts.

The challenge we face in modern life is the abundance of information, not the lack of it. Our minds are constantly fed new data, opinions, and narratives, and we need more room to process the inputs. This continuous influx can lead to a state where consumption overtakes reflection, where we're more likely to react than to think deeply. But it's crucial to recognize that genuine understanding and innovative solutions don't come from relentless information consumption or frantic activity. Wisdom comes from the deep thought that follows it.

When we make time to think and sit in quiet contemplation, insights begin to surface. These are the seeds from which solutions grow. In these moments of stillness, our minds can make connections and discover creative solutions.

In his book *Deep Work*, Cal Newport articulates this idea incredibly well.[2] He defines deep work as "the ability to focus without distraction on a cognitively demanding task." Newport argues that this focused, undistracted work is rare and valuable in our current economy, and can lead to significant productivity and satisfaction. Engaging in deep work creates the mental space necessary for complex problem-solving and innovative thinking.

Similarly, in *Stillness is the Key*, Ryan Holiday explores the power of quiet time for making better decisions and leading a fulfilling life.[3] Holiday emphasizes that stillness (the kind found in moments of solitude and reflection) is needed in order to find clarity in our chaotic world. He tells us that "stillness is what aims the archer's arrow. It inspires new ideas. It sharpens perspective and illuminates connections." I couldn't agree more.

This emphasis on contemplation is not a call to adopt religious or new-age practices, although meditation and prayer have their place in facilitating reflection. The contemplation I suggest here is practical and pragmatic. It's about carving out mental space to think deeply about issues, analyze problems without the distraction of constant input, and develop well-considered and practical solutions.

The practical implications are significant. Thinking can seem counterintuitive in a world where multitasking is glorified and being busy is worn as a badge of honor. But without deliberate thought, we become overwhelmed, stressed, and ultimately ineffective. The sheer volume and complexity of what we juggle today demand a more thoughtful approach to work and life. We must set aside time for deep work and carve out time to think. We should establish a daily habit of spending a few quiet moments in reflection before diving into the day's tasks and recognize that this thinking is not a luxury but a necessity. Thinking is hard work, but it is work worth doing.

Thinking about thinking is hard work

Exploring how we think is an essential but challenging task. It involves pausing to examine our thoughts, feelings, and beliefs, and evaluating their usefulness. Unfortunately, this isn't easy.

The process can be tricky because it requires us to be both observers and subjects. We need to be able to question our thoughts and behaviors critically while navigating our emotions and biases. It's like trying to read the fine print on a contract in a dimly lit room. You know it's important to see the details, but it's difficult to make them out.

Exploring how we think is hard because thoughts are relentless. They flow constantly; at times, it can feel like we are standing in a raging river where our thoughts are like a strong current pushing against us. As thoughts push against us at an accelerated pace, they accumulate and knock us off balance. If we lose our footing, we can get washed away and drown in the current of our thoughts.

Several years ago, I worked with a client named Jim, who struggled with an overactive mind. He was a typical executive known for his intelligence and quick thinking, but his relentless thoughts were a mixed blessing. On the one hand, Jim was insightful and innovative. He had moments of brilliance where his ideas helped the organization solve some pretty big problems. But on days when ideas and solutions came too quickly, he acted impulsively, often speaking out in meetings without fully processing his thoughts. While not inherently wrong or offensive, his quick responses undermined confidence in his strategic capabilities because many of his ideas were a swing and a miss.

As Jim's incessant thoughts spilled into conversations, his professional relationships suffered, and there was a noticeable shift in the team dynamic. He frequently interrupted others, and people felt he could never let things go. One person I interviewed described him as scatterbrained, and it was clear that others had started to resent his behavior. Jim's reputation suffered; people found him difficult to work with, and some began to avoid him.

But things turned around for Jim when he finally critically examined his thoughts. It was uncomfortable at first because Jim created a habit of expressing his thoughts out loud. However, once he realized he needed to think about his thoughts before stating them out loud, he noticed dramatic shifts in how others responded to him. By pausing to evaluate his assumptions, reframe his perspectives, and clarify his intentions, Jim's communication became more thoughtful, and his ability to influence others grew exponentially. This simple act of thinking about his thinking was the subtle shift that helped him improve his leadership effectiveness.

What do you think?

What do you think of the ideas I'm sharing with you? What are you thinking right now? And what do you think about what you are thinking? Are you aware of your thoughts or oblivious to them?

These questions are not rhetorical. They're an invitation to pause and explore your consciousness. Many of us, myself included, move through life somewhat detached from the continuous stream of thoughts that influence our feelings, decisions, and actions. We are often completely unaware of what's happening in our minds.

I remember a particular instance that highlighted this oblivion in my own life. I've always been an avid reader, finding solace and excitement in the pages of a book. One day, while reading Mortimer Adler's *How to Read a Book*, I realized something unsettling.[4] I was reading for entertainment, not for education. I skimmed the surface, consuming content without grasping the author's points. Even worse, many of the author's ideas would resonate momentarily and vanish into thin air. I'm embarrassed to admit that often, I could not recall key points from the book, even after only a few minutes.

I realized I wasn't engaging with the text at the level I needed to. But the problem was bigger. I always knew I struggled to be present with people in conversation, but now I wasn't even present when reading. It was like my mind was constantly wandering, and even though I was reading page upon page, only a fraction of the content sank in. This realization struck me as a clear example of how we can often be active without being truly present.

This experience led me to reflect on how I read and think. Just as I was reading without absorbing, I realized that often, I was thinking without understanding. My mind was busy but not productive. I consumed information without digesting it, allowing valuable insights to slip in and out of my mind too quickly.

Mortimer Adler makes a compelling point about this phenomenon in the context of reading. He argues that "a good book deserves an active reading" which goes beyond mere understanding

When we fail to think about our thinking, we let our thoughts define and control us.

to include criticism and judgment. He points out that many readers fail to analyze and interpret a book's content and give it any critical thought once they've put it down. This passive engagement with text is akin to how many engage with our thoughts. We experience them passively, letting them drift in and out of our consciousness without giving them the attention and scrutiny they deserve.

But here's the crux: just as a good book deserves an active reading, a good mind deserves an active examination. When we fail to think about our thinking, we let our thoughts define and control us without our consent. But we empower ourselves by paying attention to our thoughts, scrutinizing our beliefs, and questioning their validity. We begin to recognize patterns, identify biases, and understand the origins of our emotions and reactions.

The act of contemplation, of actively engaging with our thoughts, mirrors the rigorous analysis and critique that Adler prescribes for reading. It involves questioning what we think and why we think it. It is about challenging our assumptions, exploring alternative perspectives, and digging beneath the surface of our immediate reactions.

Reflecting on our thinking is not merely an intellectual exercise; it is a practice that strengthens mental resilience and prepares us for peak performance. This practice enhances our ability to navigate complexity, ambiguity, and the challenges of modern life. By giving our thoughts the attention they deserve, we gain the benefits of deeper understanding, improved decision-making, and a richer, more nuanced perspective on the world.

How to think about your thinking

In the early 1970s, a groundbreaking term emerged from the halls of Stanford University. The term was "metacognition", introduced by a psychologist named John Flavell.[5] Derived from the Greek "meta", meaning beyond, and "cognition", signifying thought, metacognition is the scientific term for thinking about our thinking. It became an essential field of study in the late 20th century. Its popularity grew because it shines a light on the crucial role of self-awareness and introspection in enhancing our learning, solving complex problems, and navigating the dynamics of daily life.

The idea of metacognition, while cleverly coined by Flavell, isn't new. Its roots trace back to several ancient philosophers. Socrates, known for his dialectical questioning method, started all of this in the late 5th century. Through engaging dialogues, he urged individuals to examine their beliefs and knowledge. His ancient method of inquiry, known as the Socratic method, encourages us to slow down, think, and look at our thoughts from different perspectives.[6] Perhaps that is why the Socratic method is a powerful tool in an educator's arsenal and is still used today.

Socrates wasn't alone. While he was working away in Greece during the 5th century, another philosopher five thousand miles away was promoting similar ideas. Like Socrates, the ancient Chinese philosopher Confucius believed that thinking about our thinking was essential. When he told us that "He who knows all the answers has not been asked all the questions," he spoke to the importance of slowing down to think.

So, how can we apply the wisdom of ancient philosophers and modern psychological insights to enhance our self-awareness and cognitive abilities? How do we embark on the reflective journey of thinking about our thinking?

Here are five practical strategies that you can use to think about your thinking and establish a deeper understanding and mastery of your thought processes.

PRACTICE REFLECTIVE JOURNALING

Journaling is a powerful tool for self-discovery and reflection. By maintaining a daily or weekly journal, you can create a space to express thoughts, emotions, and decisions. Writing helps uncover assumptions, clarify thoughts and feelings, and make them easier to understand and analyze. When journaling, focus on key decisions you've made, emotions you've felt, and the reasons behind your actions. Reflect on both positive experiences and challenges. Ask yourself what lessons you can learn and how you might approach similar situations differently. Over time, this practice can reveal patterns in your thinking and behavior that help you to make informed and conscious decisions.

IMPLEMENT ACTIVE QUESTIONING

The Socratic method encourages deep thinking and self-examination in groups but can be applied in solitude. Incorporate dialectical questioning into your life by asking about the validity and origins of your beliefs and decisions. Challenge yourself with questions like, "Why do I believe this?", "What evidence supports my thinking?", and "What other viewpoints should I consider?". This process helps uncover biases, assumptions, and underlying values. By actively questioning your thoughts and beliefs, you can develop a more nuanced understanding of yourself and the world around you.

PRACTICE MEDITATION

Meditation is a practice that encourages present-moment awareness and acceptance. By setting aside time each day to focus on your breath, sensations, thoughts, and feelings, you can cultivate a state of calm and clarity. Meditation practices encourage you to observe your thought patterns without judgment, enabling you to recognize habitual reactions and mental triggers. This awareness allows you to choose how you respond to thoughts and feelings, rather than reacting impulsively. As you become more familiar with your mental landscape, you'll be better equipped to navigate life's challenges with composure and insight.

SEEK OUT SUGGESTIONS

Suggestions from others can provide a fresh perspective on your thinking and behavior. Make a habit of asking for suggestions from trusted individuals, whether they are friends, family members, or colleagues. Approach these conversations with an open mind and a willingness to listen and learn.

Hearing from others can expose blind spots in your thinking and offer new insights into how others perceive you. Use this information to reflect on your actions and choose new ones. Remember, the goal of seeking suggestions is not to seek validation or feedback but to identify blind spots, consider other options and develop yourself as a person. Once you have clarity, growth gets easier.

EXPLORE DIFFERENT VIEWPOINTS

One of the most effective ways to enhance your metacognition is actively engaging with diverse perspectives. I'll discuss this in greater detail in the next chapter but for now, know that this can be achieved in many ways. Read books or articles from different genres, cultures, and viewpoints. Engage in conversations with people who have different backgrounds and experiences. Expose yourself to new and challenging situations and build a diverse network of people from whom you can learn. By considering multiple perspectives, you can broaden your understanding of complex issues and develop a more well-rounded approach to problem-solving.

Adopting several of these practices will help you think about your thinking, but adopting even one will improve your self-awareness and overall effectiveness. You'll notice sharper decision-making, increased confidence, and a clearer sense of your unique perspective and voice. This was vividly demonstrated in the case of a client I worked with several years ago, who showed me that there is a subtle but significant difference between information and wisdom.

Turning information into wisdom

Lisa is a perfect example of someone who learned to think about her thinking and reaped the rewards. With Input© as one of her top strengths on the Gallup Strengths Finder assessment, Lisa had an exceptional ability to gather and absorb data and information.[7] This skill undoubtedly contributed to her success as an executive. However, it also became her Achilles' heel. Her colleagues often perceived her as mired in minutiae, lacking strategic depth, and always looking for more information. Her penchant for details, while valuable, seemed to eclipse the bigger picture.

The turning point came during one of our sessions. Lisa frequently approached me with challenges, armed with all the necessary information, yet she struggled to resolve these issues. I noticed a pattern: she had the data but lacked the ability to act on it. It was as if collecting information was an end in itself. I prompted Lisa to consider what she thought about the information she gathered. Did she delve beyond the surface? Did she contemplate the implications and applications of this data? What was her point of view?

This line of questioning led to an epiphany for Lisa. She realized that while she excelled in gathering information, she rarely paused to reflect deeply on it. Her knowledge was abundant, but it wasn't wisdom. Lisa realized that her understanding lacked depth, and I pointed out that possessing facts was only part of the solution; applying them with mastery and skill was the real challenge.

This realization began Lisa's shift from being an information accumulator to a wise, strategic thinker. It was a subtle but substantial shift. Lisa realized that she needed to make time to think. As an executive, she was caught in a relentless cycle of problem-solving supported by the assumption that amassing information was her ticket to success. She believed that gathering knowledge, facts, and best practices would make her a more effective leader, and she discounted the idea that she could make time to truly contemplate their meaning or application.

Lisa struggled with what many of us do. She assumed that she didn't have time to think. For years, she accumulated the habits of Googling and dabbling. Whenever she had a question or an intellectual challenge to overcome, she looked outside of herself for information but never took the time to turn that knowledge into wisdom. All of that changed after she shifted her assumption about the value of information.

By engaging in the contemplative practice of coaching, Lisa began to see a new path forward. She recognized that her habits were holding her back and realized she had options. Instead of moving through her days habitually, she started to approach them consciously. Acting intentionally, she committed to making several subtle shifts.

Lisa committed to taking short 10–15-minute breaks throughout her day to reflect on the information she gathered. During these intervals, she would step away from her desk, go for a walk and ponder the information she had accumulated. She gave herself time to ask, "What do I think about this? How does this align with our goals? How can this information be applied strategically?" And it worked. By creating mental space, shifting her environment, and moving around a bit, she was able to experience a new level of thinking.

The second shift in Lisa's routine was substantially reduced internet use. She curtailed her online time, especially on social media and Google searches. Lisa likened this change to overcoming an addiction, but she soon acknowledged that she felt like she had more clarity after disconnecting from the constant stream of data. Limiting her exposure to new information allowed her the space and time necessary for deeper contemplation and understanding.

Lisa also decided to discuss her distracting desires with me and others. In our coaching sessions, she began to open up about the conflicting goals that were driving her behavior. This act of vulnerability was not easy for Lisa; it meant admitting to assumptions and biases she had long concealed. However, openly discussing them released their hold on her and helped shift her understanding of collaboration, which we agreed would play a significant role in her development. She committed to engaging more openly with her colleagues, checking her assumptions at the door, and welcoming diverse viewpoints.

Finally, Lisa took a bold step in reducing the volume of information, facts, and figures she shared in meetings and communications. This was perhaps her most challenging adjustment because it was a deeply ingrained habit. Her identity was anchored in being smart, and data was her safety net. Because she assumed that she needed numbers and facts to be credible, she had to work hard to hold back on her typical data deluge.

I encouraged Lisa to stand confidently in her perspective, and she committed to sharing her point of view rather than leaning on the points of view of others. This approach shifted how she felt about herself and very quickly shifted how others perceived her. Within months, her peers and colleagues reported that she had moved from being a data-driven manager to a thoughtful, insightful leader.

Learning from Lisa

Lisa successfully shifted her assumptions by adopting a couple of simple contemplative practices. As she integrated the practices into her life, her growth accelerated, and in less than two years she became one of the top executives in her firm. No longer submerged in a sea of unending data, she emerged as a deeply insightful leader who was more strategic and effective. Her story is an inspiration to all of us, and I wanted to share a few thoughts on what worked well for Lisa.

First, Lisa showed us that taking the time to pause and reflect doesn't have to take much time. Reflection can fit into the busiest schedules, and those who benefit most do it in short doses. Lisa didn't lock herself away for days in silent contemplation. Instead, she took short 10-15-minute breaks a few times a day to reflect and met with her coach once per month. That's it. These weren't hours-

Reflection can fit into the busiest schedules.

long, deep-diving philosophical sessions but brief strategic timeouts to reassess and regroup.

Second, Lisa didn't succumb to the inner monologue that said: "I don't have time to sit around and ponder my thoughts." That's a common pushback I hear from clients, and Lisa admitted to having this assumption. But unlike many others, Lisa didn't go so far as to dismiss deep thinking as pointless navel-gazing. She was willing to give it a try, and she took action despite her conflicting assumptions. This is a critical lesson for all of us. Change requires conscious effort and commitment, and we must remember that our assumptions don't have to drive our actions. They only drive our actions when we are unaware of them.

Third, Lisa discovered that many of her assumptions about productivity were flawed. Like many of us, Lisa was conditioned to measure her value and success by her outputs, by the tangible things she produced. She also believed what many others believe—that more hours equal productivity—prioritizing work over everything else is necessary for success, and downtime is a waste. However, once we peeled back the layers and looked at her beliefs, she recognized the flaws in her thinking. She also took to heart what Albert Einstein eloquently highlighted when he said, "We cannot solve our problems with the same thinking we used when we created them."[8]

Finally, Lisa realized that her assumptions about the value of information and data were shortsighted. For many years, Lisa prioritized information and data over insight and wisdom. It wasn't that she discounted wisdom; she just hadn't considered it before. She didn't really assume anything about wisdom—it was just a missing piece of her puzzle.

What Lisa realized, and what we all can benefit from understanding, is that information is abundant and easily accessible.[9] But information is far less valuable than wisdom. As leaders, we must realize that the real challenge lies not in acquiring information but in transforming it into actionable wisdom. This is the true benefit of contemplation—moving beyond surface-level knowledge to a deeper understanding of how to lead and succeed.

Unlike information, wisdom resides within us. It's the result of internal processing, where we connect the dots between various pieces of information and derive meaningful insights. This internalization is what differentiates a knowledgeable individual from a wise one. The knowledgeable person can recite facts and figures with ease. The wise person can apply the information in many contexts, understand its nuances, and make informed decisions. Wisdom is about moving from knowing to understanding and from data to discernment.

In a world where information is abundant, wisdom dictates how we differentiate ourselves and our actions. Actions based solely on information can often appear shallow or uninformed. In contrast, actions informed by wisdom carry a depth of understanding and conviction. They reflect an awareness of the facts and an appreciation of their significance.

Chapter Summary

- If we want to shift our assumptions, we must start by thinking about our thinking.
- Highly effective leaders make time to think. They spend time in contemplation and create mental space for strategic thinking.
- In our fast-paced world, we are often overwhelmed with information. True wisdom and effective decision-making come not from the sheer volume of data but from taking the time to process and reflect on that information.
- The practice of thinking about our thinking, or metacognition, is essential for gaining deeper insights and shifting our assumptions. It requires consciously examining our beliefs, assumptions, and mental processes.
- Practical strategies like reflective journaling, active questioning, and creating quiet time for contemplation can significantly enhance our ability to think deeply and make more informed decisions.
- By prioritizing contemplation and reflection in our daily routines, we move beyond surface-level understanding to a place of deeper wisdom, enabling us to lead with clarity and purpose.

FIVE

Collaborate: Ask Others For Help

"If I have seen further than others, it is by standing upon the shoulders of giants."
~ Isaac Newton

Before Sue became a partner, she was a standout advisor in her firm. Known for her dedication and management of client accounts, she was one of the most respected people in the business. But once she was promoted, Sue started to feel uncomfortable and realized she was treading into uncharted waters.

Taking on a partner role required Sue to expand her skill set beyond managing client money. Now, she was responsible for attracting new clients and growing the firm's business. It was a responsibility that Sue thought she wanted, but she felt overwhelmed because she was so used to the details of account management. She didn't see herself as a business development type and worried that she wouldn't be able to live up to the new expectations.

But Sue wasn't one to retreat in the face of adversity. Instead of isolating herself or blindly charging ahead, she decided to work with me as her coach. After several conversations, we arranged a meeting with the firm's CEO and a senior partner to discuss her goals and challenges around business development. It was time to address her concerns openly, seek advice, and choose a new path.

The outcome of this meeting was a game changer. The CEO and senior partner listened to Sue and offered a lot of support. They listened to her fears, asked clarifying questions, and challenged the assumptions holding her back. No one criticized her approach. They simply offered their perspectives and practical advice on navigating business development challenges. They shared that they found business development challenging when they started out and explained that Sue would learn to master this capability—just as she had mastered so many others. They also told her she didn't have to go at it alone.

Buoyed by this support and continued coaching conversations, Sue began to see her new role in a different light. The task of bringing in new business, once daunting, now appeared achievable. She started to apply what we discussed in the meeting—brokering connections, focusing on the needs of potential clients, and using the team of partners to help her through the sale. She wholeheartedly adopted a new set of assumptions about how to succeed in business development and started to see herself as a solution provider rather than a sleazy salesperson.

Sue's efforts paid off. She began to move the needle on new business and felt more confident. Her business development skills grew quickly as she built relationships based on trust and demonstrated the value that her firm could bring to prospective clients.

The results were impressive. Within three years she was consistently bringing in US$30 million in new assets under management, a testament to her hard work, adaptability, and the power of collaboration and support. To top it all off, the firm recognized her as the highest-performing partner in the business development space—all because she was able to make a few subtle but significant shifts.

How change really happens

Sue's success extended beyond the financial gains for the firm. She also significantly improved her leadership effectiveness and decisiveness scores on a 360° assessment I administered. People began to look up to her in ways they never had before, and she became a role model to many others in the firm. The CEO saw her as a go-to mentor for emerging leaders, and most importantly, she started to love her job again. What once was a source of stress turned into a source of strength, and Sue continues to make significant and sustainable strides in firm leadership.

Sue's story illustrates the power of shifting assumptions. While her results came from a shift in actions (which we will discuss in Part Three), the most profound changes came about as she reconsidered and shifted a few core assumptions that were holding her back.

Sue confronted the idea that business development was a solitary endeavor. Initially, she believed she had to shoulder the burden of attracting new clients and expanding the business independently. This perspective was daunting and isolating, making the task seem even more impossible. However, by collaborating and asking for support from others, she was able to shift her viewpoint. She realized that business development was a team effort and that leveraging her colleagues' collective experience and networks could vastly improve her chances of success. This realization allowed her to approach the task more confidently and utilize her team's strengths, which, in turn, helped her learn and grow in her new role.

Next, Sue tackled her fears and uncertainties head-on. Initially, she assumed that expressing her doubts or asking for help would be seen as weaknesses. This belief led her to internalize her struggles, making her feel even more isolated. The turning point came when she confronted her challenges by collaborating with the CEO and senior partner. When they listened to her worries and responded with support, she realized she didn't have to figure it all out alone and shifted her assumptions around what it meant to succeed at business development.

Finally, Sue's mindset shift regarding the need for perfection in her business development efforts marked a critical change in her approach. Initially, she believed that winning business required every pitch and interaction to be flawless. This assumption created immense pressure and left little room for learning and growth. However, she felt liberated when the CEO and senior partner told her that it was okay to make mistakes and that each interaction was a learning opportunity. Sue realized that business development was more about authenticity, genuine connection, and teamwork than delivering a perfect pitch. This change in perspective allowed her to engage more naturally and effectively with potential clients, leading to better outcomes.

These subtle shifts in Sue's assumptions were crucial to her growth and success. By embracing collaboration, opening up about her fears, and accepting imperfection, Sue changed her approach to business development and created remarkable results for herself and her firm. Her story is a testament to collaboration's power in shifting our assumptions and achievements.

Birds of a feather flock together

Entrepreneur and author Jim Rohn is often quoted as saying we are the average of the five people we spend the most time with. The idea is that our social circles significantly influence who we are and who we become. But how much can the people closest to us shape our thinking, behavior, and overall outlook on life? How much truth is there to this statement, and what does it mean for us practically?

Research in social psychology and behavioral science suggests there's a significant amount of truth to Rohn's statement. The beliefs, attitudes, and behaviors of those we interact with frequently can seep into our thinking, often without our conscious awareness. This phenomenon, known as social influence, can impact everything from our self-esteem and stress levels, to our lifestyle choices and professional ambitions.

Studies have demonstrated that if we are surrounded by individuals who prioritize healthy living, we're more likely to adopt similar behaviors.[1] Conversely, if our close friends or family have unhealthy habits or pessimistic attitudes, we might also find these traits rubbing off on us. That doesn't mean we're simply puppets of our environment, rather, it highlights the importance of being mindful about who we spend our time with.

The emotional and psychological impact of our social networks can't be understated. Being around positive, supportive individuals can improve mental and emotional well-being, while the opposite can increase stress and negativity. The quality of our relationships plays a crucial role in our overall happiness and satisfaction with life.

Take my friend Steve, who exemplifies the powerful influence of a social circle. Steve's career began on a positive note. When he first joined the company, he was enthusiastic, energetic, and incredibly positive. His enthusiasm was infectious, and his rapid ascent from team leader to vice president within five years was a testament to his leadership and the high regard in which he was held.

However, the higher Steve climbed on the corporate ladder, the heavier the burden of stress became. Steve began to release his stress by venting with others in the business. Initially, his complaints and frustrations seemed like a harmless way to blow off steam. Yet, over time, his venting transformed into pervasive negativity. What was once a source of relief turned into a bad habit, and Steve's continuous negativity eventually led to his demotion.

When Steve was demoted, he was humiliated and struggled to understand why. Thankfully, his boss had an open and honest conversation with him and pointed out that his negative energy had become a drain on the team. His boss also highlighted that his association with a group known for complaining had not gone unnoticed.

Reflecting on his situation, Steve realized that his boss was right. His so-called "venting sessions" with the company complainers had morphed into a pattern of negativity that infected his reputation. What once seemed like a harmless habit became a defining trait, and he admitted that he was at fault. He also acknowledged that the miserable energy of his companions rubbed off on him. Engaging in venting sessions with this group allowed others to influence him in ways he hadn't anticipated. Steve realized that his attitude and behaviors were contagious, as were those of the folks he associated with. By spending time with the group of complainers, he was throwing fuel on the fire and making the problem worse.

Caught in a cult

Steve's story serves as a cautionary tale about the importance of maintaining a positive social circle. It illustrates how others can subtly influence our lives, alter our attitudes, and stunt our professional and personal growth. Nowhere is this more visible than in cults. Cults are often known for the charismatic leaders who start them, but the community plays a significant part in embedding assumptions into the psyche of its victims.[2]

While cults are a dramatic illustration of how a group of people can significantly reshape an individual's beliefs, they are accurate. By employing complex psychological, social, and emotional tactics to indoctrinate and retain members, cult leaders—and the people who follow them—manipulate individuals into believing some pretty crazy things.

Initially, individuals may be drawn to cults in search of community, belonging, or purpose, especially during vulnerable periods. This sense of connection and understanding is compelling, offering solace and answers during uncertainty or loneliness. Once engaged, newcomers often experience something called "love bombing", where they are showered with flattery, affection, and attention. This process makes individuals feel uniquely special and valued, deepening their attachment to the group and its members. It is a deceptive form of persuasion that masks the group's ulterior motives with a facade of care and camaraderie.

The journey into the heart of a cult is gradual; initial teachings and practices may appear harmless or align with personal beliefs. However, these can evolve into more extreme, isolating doctrines. This slow indoctrination process prevents the sudden recognition of the shift from moderate to radical ideologies.

Isolation from people outside of the cult is a critical strategy—cults may encourage or enforce separation from family, friends, and society to gain control. This isolation can be physical, but it is often psychological. It fosters a sense of us vs. them that discourages trust in external sources and tightens the group's grip on the individual's worldview. As dependency deepens, the cult assumes control over many aspects of members' lives, including how they spend their time, the information they consume, and, in some cases, their finances. This comprehensive control reinforces members' reliance on the group for their social, emotional, and material needs.

Identity transformation is another powerful mechanism cults use to redefine your sense of self in terms of group ideology and hierarchy. This new identity can erode previous social roles and self-concepts, making the group an integral part of the individual's identity.

Cults also leverage fear and guilt effectively, using them as tools to retain and control members. Fear of external threats, spiritual ruin, or expulsion from the group can paralyze members with anxiety, while guilt about past actions or doubts can compel conformity and silence criticism.

Understanding the mechanisms by which cults manipulate and control provides insight into the broader impacts of social influence. It underscores the need for vigilance in our social connections and adopted assumptions. It also highlights the importance of maintaining autonomy, critical thinking, and healthy, supportive social environments.

What's holding you back

What can we learn from people like Sue, Jim Rohn, my friend Steve, and those lured into cults? Social influence is a powerful force that can trap us horribly in a wicked cult or positively in a highly effective team. Some might consider it a scary factor littered with risk, but I believe the opposite is true.

We must be open to social influence to learn, grow, and be the best versions of ourselves. We must connect and collaborate with others if we want to shift our assumptions because, left to our own devices, we will either fail to adapt or adapt too slowly. We need to be aware of the risks involved in social influence but accept the risks if we want to reach our goals and grow as individuals.

A wonderful poem, *There's a Hole in My Sidewalk* by Portia Nelson, illustrates how difficult it can be to learn and grow when we operate in isolation.[3] This piece, though simple in its structure, is profound in its message and is something I believe everyone should revisit regularly. The poem goes as follows:

I walk down the street.
There is a deep hole in the sidewalk.
I fall in.
I am lost...
I am helpless.
It isn't my fault.
It takes forever to find a way out.

I walk down the same street.
There is a deep hole in the sidewalk.
I pretend I don't see it.
I fall in again.
I can't believe I am in the same place.
But, it isn't my fault.
It still takes me a long time to get out.

I walk down the same street.
There is a deep hole in the sidewalk.
I see it is there.
I still fall in.
It's a habit.
My eyes are open.
I know where I am.
It is my fault.
I get out immediately.

I walk down the same street.
There is a deep hole in the sidewalk.
I walk around it.
I walk down another street.

This poem offers a powerful metaphor for navigating life's challenges. As the poet so eloquently shows us, humans often stumble into mistakes, and remain blind to their patterns. Over time, we recognize the traps but fall into them anyway—out of habit or denial. True change begins only when we take ownership of our actions, consciously avoid the pitfalls, and eventually forge an entirely new path.

Portia Nelson's poem is regularly used in leadership and personal development training across the country, illustrating self-awareness, accountability, adaptability, and the transformative power of choice. We learn to see our patterns, take responsibility for our actions, and make deliberate decisions to change. Growth, after all, is not about perfection—it's about progress, one conscious step at a time.

But here's what often gets missed by the masses. Change doesn't have to be so complicated. We've built a cultural narrative that frames growth as hard, slow, and painful—a grind rather than a subtle, natural process. Interpretations of this poem, while insightful, often reinforce this myth. Yet growth can be simple if we attempt it with people walking by our side.

A better way forward

Thankfully, repeatedly falling into a hole is not the only narrative available. There is a better way to learn and grow—if we are willing to look for it.

Imagine instead that you are walking down a street that is busy and bustling with people. In this scenario, if there was a gaping hole in the ground, do you think you would fall into it? Surely, someone would point it out. A kind soul would stand beside the hole and warn others of its existence. Another would likely call the Department of Public Works and demand that the hole be fixed immediately. People would rally, get their hands on some caution tape, and put barriers around that hole because no one wants to see someone fall into it.

People are inherently good, and when we approach life like the big collaboration that it is, we reduce stress, accelerate our growth, and improve our experience.

The truth is that we often fall into holes because we walk alone. When we isolate ourselves from others, we take on significant risks and slow down our learning and growth. Other people can offer perspectives, wisdom, and insights that we might miss or overlook when we move through life alone. They can warn us of the holes ahead, help us out when we fall into them, and guide us toward safer, more fruitful paths.

This realization brings us to an essential shift in our assumptions. Personal growth, leadership, and change aren't solo sports; they're a team effort. Once we see things this way, we realize how important it is to consciously connect with others and approach our lives as a collaboration. From this perspective, we are not isolated individuals navigating the world alone but parts of a greater whole, contributing to and benefiting from the wisdom of the community.

By acknowledging that we are the sum of our relationships, we open ourselves up to a richer, more interconnected experience of growth. That does not mean that we lose our sense of self or individuality. The focus here is on enhancing our lives by opening to the insights, support, and compassion of others. It's about recognizing that our paths are interwoven and that by connecting with others, we improve our odds.

So, as we move forward, we should stop walking down the streets of our lives with blinders on. Instead, we should open our eyes and hearts to the people around us, recognizing that every interaction

Personal growth, leadership, and change aren't solo sports.

holds the potential for growth. By embracing the collective wisdom of our communities, we can avoid many of the holes that once trapped us and pave new roads to places we once thought unreachable. It is a crucial concept for anyone who wants to shift their assumptions—don't try to do it alone. Success is not a solo sport.

Cultivating collaboration

We can't do it alone, so we must intentionally cultivate collaboration. That means actively seeking out individuals who complement us, challenge us, and share our commitment to learning and growth. Building such a team requires more than just gathering skilled people; it involves nurturing an environment where open communication, mutual respect, and shared responsibility are the norm. It's about recognizing that everyone we meet brings value and that together, we can tackle challenges more creatively and effectively than we ever could alone.

The process involved in building your team is beyond the scope of this book, but I want to provide a few suggestions to get you started. To begin, reach out to those whose work and values resonate with you, as well as those who don't. It is essential to consider alternative perspectives so you don't create an echo chamber. Join groups and forums where interests align, but perspectives diverge. Participate in events that draw a crowd you can connect to. The aim is to create connections with people you can turn to, not just for their knowledge or skills, but for their ability to question and widen your thinking. This task requires a deliberate effort to engage and nurture relationships grounded in mutual respect and shared curiosity. As you begin to act, remember that the richness of your network is not just in the numbers but in the depth and quality of your connections.

We aren't simply looking to expand our connections on LinkedIn or some other social media platform. We are trying to build real, human connections.

Now, let me round out this chapter with a crucial point. Collaboration can indeed help us make subtle shifts in our assumptions, but subtle shifts in our assumptions are also needed to activate the power of collaboration. To collaborate, we must change the way we think and allow collaboration to influence our thoughts. If you are ready to start the process, here are four core assumptions that we can change to allow for more collaboration.

ASSUMPTION #1: I CANNOT TRUST OTHERS.

The assumption that "I cannot trust others" and its cousin, "It's easier to do it myself," are beliefs I find in many of my clients. It burdens its host with unnecessary stress and keeps us from being our best.

The belief that we cannot trust others directly reflects the distracting desire for control addressed earlier in this book. When we constantly try to control everything by maintaining a tight grip on every aspect of a task, we tend to do so because we don't trust. Shifting away from this belief involves recognizing the strength in vulnerability and the power of delegation. Trusting others and sharing responsibilities can create outcomes that are better than what we can achieve alone. Beginning with minor tasks and gradually increasing trust can pave the way for a stronger team dynamic.

ASSUMPTION #2: I NEED TO OUTTHINK OTHERS.

This belief is equally troubling. When we believe we need to outthink others, we foster a competitive environment that stunts personal and social growth. This assumption is tied to the need to be right, introduced in Chapter Two, and overshadows the value of collective intelligence. By embracing a collaborative mindset, where the goal is to reach the best outcome together, we open ourselves to a wealth of knowledge and perspectives. Recognizing that each team member brings unique insights can enrich our understanding and solutions.

ASSUMPTION #3: I NEED TO AVOID CONFLICT.

Assuming that we need to avoid conflict, mistakes harmony for the absence of disagreement. This view often leads to missed opportunities for critical discussions that can spur growth and innovation and improve our outcomes. This aversion to conflict is linked to the need to be safe, driving individuals away from potentially uncomfortable but necessary conversations. Shifting this assumption means viewing conflict as an opportunity for development. Constructive conflict, grounded in respectful communication, can lead to more robust and well-considered decisions.

ASSUMPTION #4: I NEED TO PLEASE OTHERS.

The need to please others leads us to compromise too quickly. This belief reflects the distracting desire to be liked, often at the expense of your contributions. Recognizing that respect and mutual understanding are the cornerstones of collaboration creates a setting where all ideas are considered and valued. Asserting our ideas while being open to others' perspectives creates an environment where diverse viewpoints are tolerated and celebrated, enhancing the collaborative spirit.

Chapter Summary

- Success often comes from collaboration rather than solitary effort. Asking for help and leveraging the collective wisdom of others can create significant breakthroughs.

- Collaboration begins by recognizing that we don't have to—and shouldn't—go at it alone. Seeking support and advice from others allows us to navigate new challenges efficiently and confidently.

- Collaboration can help us shift our assumptions. When we collaborate, we expose our beliefs, open ourselves to learning, and challenge ourselves to grow.

- Building strong professional relationships and relying on our team's strengths can transform daunting tasks into achievable goals, leading to greater success and fulfillment.

- Embracing the idea that we are stronger together than alone can dramatically enhance our effectiveness and lead to significant personal and professional growth.

SIX

Update: Embrace Empowering Assumptions

"Progress is impossible without change, and those who cannot change their minds cannot change anything."
~ George Bernard Shaw

I've always been a fan of the Renaissance mathematician and astronomer Nicolaus Copernicus. And for good reason. For centuries, people believed the Earth sat still at the center of the universe while everything else—the Sun, Moon, and stars—revolved around it. That assumption was comfortable, unquestioned, and, as it turns out, completely wrong.

Nicolaus Copernicus noticed something was off, and he questioned it. The planets' movements didn't align with the story everyone accepted, so he got curious instead of brushing aside his doubts. He observed. He calculated. And he came to a startling conclusion: the Earth wasn't the center of the universe. It moved, orbiting the Sun like the other planets.

That idea—so simple, yet so disruptive—upended everything. It challenged not just science but the very assumptions people built their worldview on. And here's the thing: challenging assumptions wasn't safe. Copernicus knew his findings would invite ridicule and resistance. But he published anyway, sparking a revolution in how we see the world.[1]

What Copernicus did goes beyond astronomy; he showed us the power of questioning assumptions. He taught us that the beliefs we don't examine limit us and keep us stuck in outdated ways of thinking. Growth comes when we're willing to reexamine the things we've always taken for granted and replace them with ideas that move us forward.

The courage to change

Copernicus didn't just kick off a scientific revolution; he demonstrated a way to show up in this world. By questioning established truths, he reshaped the field of astronomy and the broader canvas of human thought. For many, this is the central theme of the story. Copernicus represents the archetype of the innovator, an individual whose intellectual firepower creates breakthroughs that transcend the boundaries of their specific disciplines. A closer look reveals something much more intriguing.

Human beings look up to people like Copernicus because they push the boundaries of what we know and challenge us to think differently. There is something about creative genius that resonates with all of us. Innovators force us to confront the limitations of our current understanding and inspire us to move into uncharted territories. They are celebrated for their intellectual achievements and role in driving human progress, but their gravitas seduces us.

Throughout history, thought leaders like Galileo, Newton, and Einstein asked big questions and introduced novel theories that challenged the status quo. Galileo laid the groundwork for modern science and technology. Newton helped us understand the modern world by introducing the laws of motion and his mathematical law of gravitation. Einstein's theory of relativity showed us that space and time are interconnected and relative. But Copernicus's story is more interesting because fundamentally, it is a story about courage.

In the 16th century, the church was the gatekeeper of knowledge. The church leaders believed they were the purveyors of truth, so Copernicus's heliocentric theory—the very idea that the Earth revolved around the Sun—upended the church's truth. To question what the church had to say was more than heretical; it was dangerous, and Copernicus knew that defying religious doctrine could lead to public condemnation, professional ruin, or even death.

But he published his findings anyway, and the rest is history. Copernicus secured his legacy but did so in a way that contributed to society and advanced humanity. Today, we still reap the benefits of the courageous steps he took.

Leaving a legacy

Copernicus's story reminds us that history is written by those willing to stand between the known and the unknown. It is shaped by those brave enough to question the certainties of their time and propose a new path forward. Progress takes just one voice to change the collective belief. Once changed, we can never return to the old way of thinking. Victor Hugo said it best when he told us that "no army can stop an idea whose time has come."[2]

Legacies are built in the moments when someone chooses growth over comfort and curiosity over certainty. The most impactful individuals question what others take for granted, constantly refining their understanding and adapting to new challenges. Growth isn't a one-time event—it's a way of living.

Trailblazers lead by testing limits and pushing beyond what's familiar. They rarely settle for the status quo and seem to hate conventional wisdom—they test it, challenge it, and welcome ideas that move beyond it. This openness transforms life into an ongoing process of intentional choices that create momentum and meaning. Figures like Copernicus understood this and left a legacy because they chose to do so.

People like Nelson Mandela, Marie Curie, Martin Luther King Jr., and several other great leaders I mentioned throughout this book refused to accept the world as it was handed to them. Instead, they questioned, reimagined, and reshaped it. Mandela envisioned equality triumphing over oppression and worked for years to make that vision a reality. Curie ventured into the mysteries of radioactivity, undeterred by the risks. King dreamed of a reality where justice prevailed over division and pushed against boundaries that only the most tenacious and resilient could withstand. Each of these men and women left a legacy and created a better world because they dared to update their assumptions despite the so-called prevailing knowledge.

Trailblazers lead
by testing limits.

Refining your philosophy

What is your philosophy on life? What assumptions do you hold near and dear, and what would happen if you updated them? Do you assume the world is working for you, or do you feel it constantly works against you? Do you believe you are the master of your destiny, or do you have this crushing feeling that you'll never get what you want? Do you think you can have what you want or don't deserve to live a happy and meaningful life? The way you answer such questions really matters.

I wrote earlier that we need to think about our thinking and ask others for help, but those actions are only the tip of the iceberg. To truly shift our assumptions, we must look beneath the surface at our internal operating system and update the assumptions that hold us back. We must embrace empowering beliefs and ultimately shift our assumptions away from those that limit us. Updating how we think and our beliefs is the engine that drives our actions.

Several years before I started my business, I was a senior leader in a government organization, and quite honestly, I felt like a bureaucrat. Going to work every day felt like pushing a boulder uphill, and even though I cared about the work I was doing and tried hard to keep the fire burning, I felt a bit empty inside. The emptiness led me to pursue a new career, but moving from the stable, structured environment inside the U. S. Federal Government wasn't easy.

I carried a wide array of assumptions about what success looked like. I believed a higher authority should validate decisions before implementation, so I spent too much time looking outside myself for suggestions and answers. This tendency to seek external approval slowed my decision-making and stifled my creativity and independence. This approach may have been necessary in a government role where procedures and protocols dominate, but in the entrepreneurial world, it proved to be a significant handicap. The dynamic nature of the business required a shift towards more autonomous decision-making, and I felt ill-equipped.

Additionally, I believed that I should maintain formal structures in professional interactions. This assumption led me to operate in a way that wasn't conducive to the fluid and often informal nature of the markets I wanted to serve. Instead of leveraging flexibility and speed, I built unnecessary barriers that complicated direct communication and quick decision-making, slowing down potential business opportunities and sales processes.

Another deep-seated belief was that clients should seek me out based on my reputation and previous achievements. This passive approach to business development meant I didn't actively or effectively market myself or my new venture. As a result, I inadvertently hid my services from the market, waiting for opportunities to come to me rather than proactively creating those opportunities. This strategy was far from effective in the competitive and noisy marketplace and needed a radical overhaul.

Furthermore, I carried over the assumption from my government role that changes within an organization needed to be implemented like a major initiative—systematically and with heavy top-down management. This perspective was not aligned with the more agile and responsive approach required in a smaller, more dynamic business environment. My advice to clients often mirrored this outdated view, which was inconsistent with the evolving needs of businesses and contradictory to the principles of subtle, incremental changes that I now advocate in this book.

The shift in my assumptions was pivotal, but it happened gradually. I learned to trust my judgment and make decisions more independently, adapting to a business's fast-paced and unpredictable nature. I embraced a more casual and direct form of communication with team members and clients, which fostered stronger relationships and quicker resolutions. I also revamped my marketing approach, becoming more proactive in reaching out to potential clients and promoting my services, significantly increasing my visibility and business growth.

Ultimately, my experience moving from the bureaucracy of the Federal Government to running my practice taught me that success in a new field demands a shift in how we think about work and achievement. Letting go of outdated beliefs and finding empowering assumptions were crucial steps in creating a new career and a thriving business.

Updating your beliefs

One of the most interesting things I've learned from twenty-five years in leadership and a decade of coaching leaders is that many of us share assumptions. That is particularly true when the assumptions are negative or disempowering. Disempowering beliefs often cluster around fears and limitations, creating a self-fulfilling prophecy that restricts personal and organizational growth.

If we want to update our assumptions, we must take a long, hard look at them and explore empowering alternatives. Twelve negative assumptions consistently pop up and are directly tied to the four core cravings discussed in Chapter Two. In the next section, you'll see these alongside empowering alternatives. Use these to shift your assumptions.

THE DESIRE TO CONTROL

Assumption #1: Things will go wrong if I don't control every detail.

This belief leads to micromanagement, where you feel compelled to oversee every minor detail, ultimately stifling your creativity and initiative. Such behavior puts a burden on you that is difficult to manage, causing unnecessary stress and preventing those around you from developing and taking ownership. This mindset can strain relationships and inhibit personal growth, stopping others from learning and contributing effectively.

Empowering alternatives

1. **I can trust and rely on other people.** When we delegate and trust others, we create opportunities for collaboration and shared ownership, often leading to better results. Allowing others to contribute helps them build their confidence and it reduces our stress.

2. **Things will go wrong despite my best efforts.** When we accept that mistakes are inevitable, we can focus on solutions rather than dwelling on fear or blame. This perspective helps us build resilience and adaptability, allowing us to learn from setbacks and continue moving forward.

3. **My value lies in my leadership, not my control.** Great leaders guide, inspire, and support rather than micromanage. When we focus on the bigger picture and empower others to take responsibility, we amplify our impact and create a culture of trust and innovation.

Assumption #2: My value is linked to how much control I have.

Linking your self-worth directly to control over external circumstances leads to constant anxiety and feelings of inadequacy. The truth is that we are constantly up against unpredictable situations, and we must be able to adapt. When you tie your value to your ability to control everything around you, you set yourself up for disappointment and stress, as no one can control every variable all the time. This belief can also strain relationships, as it may cause you to be overly critical or demanding of others.

Empowering alternatives

1. **I am inherently valuable.** When we recognize that our worth comes from within and is not tied to control or external achievements, we experience peace, confidence, and composure. This understanding frees us to approach challenges with self-acceptance, fostering healthier relationships and greater emotional resilience.

2. **Letting go of control doesn't diminish my value—it enhances it.** When we release the need to control every aspect of our environment, we create space for trust, collaboration, and personal growth. Letting go allows us to focus on our strengths and contributions, which amplifies our impact and deepens our connections with others.

3. **My true value lies in my contributions, character, and the positive impact I make on others.** When we focus on what we can give rather than what we can control, we build a stable sense of self-worth that isn't tied to external circumstances. By emphasizing the positive effects of

our actions and the strength of our character, we create a foundation of value that can withstand the unpredictability of life.

Assumption #3: Being in control will keep me safe.

This belief can trap you in constant vigilance and anxiety, making relaxing and enjoying the present moment difficult. When we assume that we must be in control to be safe, we create unnecessary constraints and hold ourselves back. That leads to a rigid and overly cautious life, where opportunities for growth and joy are missed. Over time, this mindset limits our ability to take meaningful risks, build deeper connections, and have new experiences. Instead of creating safety, it triggers a false sense of security that keeps us stuck and unfulfilled.

Empowering alternatives

1. **Uncertainty can lead to unexpected opportunities.** We create room for growth and discovery when we accept that not everything can be controlled and that uncertainty is a natural part of life. Embracing the unknown opens us to experiences and possibilities that can enrich our lives in ways we never imagined.

2. **Being connected will keep me safe.** When we focus on building strong relationships and a supportive network, we create a foundation of trust and security that control cannot provide. Relying on meaningful connections helps us feel grounded and supported, knowing we are not alone in facing life's challenges.

3. **Safety comes from flexibility, not control.** Just as a muscle must be flexible to prevent injury, emotional safety comes from emotional flexibility. If we are too rigid in our thinking, we will feel threatened and unsafe and try desperately to control the uncontrollable.

THE NEED TO BE RIGHT

Assumption #4: Admitting I'm wrong will make me appear weak or unintelligent.

This assumption can hold you back by preventing you from acknowledging mistakes. It creates a fear-driven environment where you and those around you may be reluctant to admit errors. This lack of transparency can lead to missed opportunities for improvement while stifling innovation and progress. Furthermore, it can cause you to miss out on valuable insights and feedback from others, as they may be hesitant to share their perspectives.

Empowering alternatives

1. **Admitting mistakes is a strength that fosters trust and continuous learning.** We demonstrate courage and integrity when we acknowledge our mistakes. We create an atmosphere of trust and openness and encourage those around us to view errors as opportunities for learning and growth. Ultimately, we promote a culture of resilience and improvement.

2. **Vulnerability leads to deeper connections and personal growth.** When we allow ourselves to be vulnerable, we create space for authentic connections and mutual

respect. Admitting our faults builds empathy, strengthens relationships, and helps create an environment where everyone feels safe to contribute and grow.

3. **Acknowledging mistakes enhances credibility.** Owning our errors shows that we value honesty over the illusion of perfection. This transparency builds trust and strengthens our reputation as reliable, accountable, and committed to growth.

Assumption #5: I must win every argument.

When you feel that you must win every argument, it can lead to unnecessary conflict and strained professional and personal relationships. This mindset reduces your ability to empathize and consider other viewpoints, which are critical components of effective communication. It can create an environment where discussions turn into battles, leaving little room for mutual understanding or growth. This approach damages relationships and stifles your personal development.

Empowering alternatives

1. **Understanding is more important than winning.** Focusing on understanding rather than proving a point creates space for meaningful dialogue and mutual respect. This shift helps us learn from others' perspectives and expand our understanding.

2. **Listening and learning from others enriches my perspective.** When we approach disagreements as opportunities to learn and grow, we turn conflict into a chance to broaden our horizons. Active listening helps us

gain valuable insights, build stronger problem-solving skills, and form more empathetic and supportive relationships.

3. **Strengthening a relationship is more valuable than winning an argument.** Prioritizing relationships over being right builds trust and goodwill and strengthens relationships. Doing so creates better results over time.

Assumption #6: Others will respect me more if I am right.

People don't respect you because you are right. They respect you because of your willingness to listen, learn, and value contributions. The need to always be right can alienate others and inhibit meaningful collaboration. It often prevents you from engaging in discussions that could lead to innovative solutions. This mindset can create a barrier to effective communication and teamwork, discouraging open dialogue and diverse perspectives. Ultimately, it can lead to a lack of trust and respect from those around you, as they may feel undervalued and unheard.

Empowering alternatives

1. **Being open to learning earns respect.** Approaching conversations with a willingness to learn demonstrates humility and curiosity that naturally builds respect. By valuing others' insights, we create an environment where people feel appreciated, fostering collaboration and mutual trust.

2. **Valuing others' contributions strengthens our team.** Acknowledging and appreciating others' contributions inspires others to bring their best ideas forward. This elevates team morale and boosts performance.

3. **Respect comes from trust, not being right.** Many people misunderstand where respect comes from. By focusing on trust rather than winning debates, we create stronger relationships and pave the way for lasting partnerships.

THE NEED TO BE SAFE

Assumption #7: Sticking to what I know and avoiding risks is the best way to stay safe.

This overly cautious approach can limit personal and professional development by avoiding new challenges and opportunities. While familiarity provides comfort, it often leads to stagnation. By staying within your comfort zone, you miss out on the growth and revitalization that come from exploring new experiences and taking calculated risks. This mindset can prevent you from reaching your full potential and discovering new passions or skills.

Empowering alternatives

1. **Expanding your capabilities and taking risks is the best way to stay safe.** We increase our flexibility and resilience when we step out of our comfort zones. Like a muscle stretched and strengthened, we end up better equipped to handle the stresses and strains of life.
2. **Taking risks leads to greater rewards and learning.** Risk-taking is often the catalyst for progress. Even when risks don't lead to immediate success, the lessons we gain strengthen our ability to grow and improve over time.
3. **Staying curious and adaptable ensures long-term safety.** Curiosity keeps us engaged. Adaptability allows us to pivot.

Together, these qualities help us confidently move through uncertainty, making us more resilient and prepared for the unexpected.

Assumption #8: Something terrible will happen if I don't protect myself and others.

Living in constant fear of potential dangers can significantly detract from your quality of life and inhibit your ability to take calculated risks that could lead to rewarding experiences. This mindset can lead to excessive caution, preventing you from fully engaging in life and exploring new opportunities. It creates a barrier to personal growth and fulfillment, as the fear of potential harm overshadows the potential for positive outcomes.

Empowering alternatives

1. **Balanced caution is the way to go.** Take a measured approach to risk. Don't go in with blinders on, but also don't be petrified of disasters that likely won't happen.
2. **Good and bad things happen regardless of what I do.** Acknowledging that some events are beyond our control helps us release the burden of constant vigilance. Focusing on what we can influence and letting go of the rest creates more room for peace, growth, and enjoyment.
3. **True protection comes from preparation, not fear.** Preparation helps us to face challenges with confidence and composure. By preparing, we turn potential dangers into manageable situations.

Assumption #9: It's better to be overly cautious than face the unknown.

This belief leads to missed opportunities and can cause you to remain in your comfort zone, avoiding the unknown rather than embracing it as a chance for growth. Clinging to excessive caution may feel like a protective measure, but it often stifles innovation and personal development. The comfort of familiar routines may give you a sense of security but can also lead to stagnation. Over time, this mindset makes you miss out on opportunities for learning and development, leaving you unfulfilled and stuck in a boring routine.

Empowering alternatives

1. **Stepping into the unknown is an opportunity for growth.** When we embrace uncertainty, we open ourselves to experiences that challenge and expand our capabilities. By stepping beyond what's familiar, we discover new strengths and possibilities that can lead to personal and professional breakthroughs.
2. **Caution should be balanced with curiosity.** While caution helps us avoid unnecessary risks, curiosity drives us to explore, innovate, and grow. By balancing these two forces, we can take thoughtful steps into the unknown, creating opportunities while staying mindful of potential challenges.
3. **Exploring the unknown builds resilience and confidence.** When we face the unknown head-on, we develop the skills and self-assurance needed to adapt to life's uncertainties. Each step we take into uncharted territory strengthens our ability to handle whatever comes next.

THE NEED TO BE LIKED

Assumption #10: I must please everyone to be liked and accepted.

This assumption can cause you to stretch yourself too thin, trying to meet everyone's expectations at the expense of your own needs and happiness. It often leads to resentment and burnout, as prioritizing others leaves little time for self-care and personal growth. Additionally, this mindset can result in losing authenticity, as you may find yourself conforming to others' desires rather than staying true to your values and beliefs.

Empowering alternatives

1. **I can respect others' opinions without needing to conform to them.** When we honor different viewpoints without sacrificing our values, we create relationships built on mutual respect rather than approval. This approach allows us to stay authentic while fostering more meaningful and satisfying connections.

2. **Others' approval does not define my worth.** Recognizing that our value is intrinsic frees us from the exhausting need to meet everyone's expectations. By focusing on what truly matters to us, we can confidently pursue our goals and build relationships that value who we genuinely are.

3. **Being authentic attracts the right connections.** If we prioritize authenticity over people-pleasing, we naturally attract those who appreciate us for who we are. This alignment creates deeper, more rewarding relationships while allowing us to focus on what makes us truly happy and fulfilled.

Assumption #11: How much others approve of me determines my worth.

Relying on external validation for self-esteem is unstable and unsustainable. It can lead to constant anxiety and a diminished sense of self-worth as you search for approval from others. This dependence on external validation can cause you to lose sight of your values and achievements, making it challenging to develop a stable and confident sense of self. Moreover, it can result in a cycle of people-pleasing behavior, where you prioritize others' opinions over your own needs and desires.

Empowering alternatives

1. **My self-worth is based on my standards and achievements.** When we define our value by our standards and efforts, we create a stable foundation for self-esteem that isn't swayed by external opinions. This perspective allows us to focus on our personal growth and successes, building confidence from within.

2. **I am inherently valuable.** We break free from needing constant approval when we realize our value is inherent. This belief provides a deep sense of peace and security, enabling us to appreciate our unique qualities and navigate life authentically and clearly.

3. **My worth is defined by how I live, not how I'm perceived.** When we focus on living in alignment with our values and purpose, we stop chasing the fleeting approval of others. This mindset allows us to create a life of meaning and fulfillment.

Assumption #12: If someone dislikes me, something must be wrong with me.

This assumption can be damaging to your self-esteem and inhibit authentic self-expression. Believing that you must be flawed if someone dislikes you can lead to constant self-doubt and a tendency to change yourself to please others. This mindset can prevent you from being your true self, as you may constantly seek approval and validation from others rather than embracing your unique qualities and strengths.

Empowering alternatives

1. **Not everyone has to like me, and that is okay.** Accepting that differing opinions and preferences are a natural part of life releases us from the need for universal approval. We build stronger, more authentic relationships when we stop chasing people and trying to win them over.

2. **When someone dislikes me, it reflects more about them than me.** Negative opinions and judgments often come from one's insecurities or biases. When people dislike us, they are often projecting those insecurities onto us.

3. **My value isn't defined by others' opinions.** When we focus on our intrinsic worth and the qualities that make us unique, we stop seeking validation from others. This perspective helps us build a stable sense of self that isn't easily shaken, creating a foundation for a balanced and fulfilling life.

Chapter Summary

- Our success is limited by the assumptions we fail to challenge.

- The courage to question widely accepted truths and deeply held beliefs is essential for personal and professional growth. It allows us to break free from constraints and explore new possibilities.

- Individuals who lead truly impactful lives understand the importance of questioning and refining their assumptions.

- People tend to adopt twelve core assumptions. Each is directly tied to the core cravings we discussed in Chapter Two.

- Seeing how each assumption ties into our core cravings makes it clear how they hold us back. By updating these assumptions and letting go of those distractions, we can improve our performance and find a better way forward.

PART 3

Shifting Actions

SEVEN

Formulate: Start with Strategy

"Tactics without strategy is the noise before defeat."
~ Sun Tzu

In the spring of 1963, Martin Luther King Jr. found himself locked up in a Birmingham jail. He was arrested for parading without a permit, but everyone knew the charges were a sham. It was an important moment in the civil rights movement, and King's adversaries were out to get him. Once arrested, he was placed in solitary confinement and denied the legal counsel that he deserved.

After President John F. Kennedy intervened several days later, King was granted access to his lawyer, Clarence Jones. Jones had a gift for King as the nation watched, some with bated breath and others with skepticism. He handed him a local newspaper that printed an open letter criticizing King and denouncing his tactics as "unwise and untimely". The eight white clergymen who wrote the letter urged the African American community to be patient and rely on courtroom battles rather than street protests.[1] But King saw through the veil of these criticisms and decided to write a rebuttal.

With nothing but the newspaper margins to initially write on, King began crafting a response. When he ran out of space, he wrote on scraps of paper. Eventually, his lawyer was able to smuggle in a notebook so King could finish his masterpiece. After several days of working feverishly, his "Letter from a Birmingham Jail" was complete. It became a manifesto on justice, civil rights, and the moral imperative for nonviolent resistance.[2]

In his letter, King explained the urgency of action and countered the clergy's call for patience with a profound truth: "Justice too long delayed is justice denied." He wrote with an impeccable tone and made a strong case for immediate change. He challenged the complacency of those more comfortable with order than justice and elevated the conversation by focusing on higher principles like morality, justice, and nonviolent action.

King's letter was an outstanding defense of the Birmingham campaign, but it was so much more. In just seven thousand words, he clearly stated the movement's intent and outlined a strategy for future civil rights endeavors. Using his time in jail to write down his vision, turned a moment of seeming defeat into a decisive victory for the civil rights movement.

After his release, he went on to lead over 200,000 people to march on Washington, where he delivered his iconic "I Have a Dream" speech. The Civil Rights Act was passed shortly after that. Time Magazine selected him as its Person of the Year, and the Nobel Peace Prize was awarded to King for his steadfast advocacy and leadership.

Strategy before action

When it comes to change, the sequence of actions can mean the difference between success and failure. The narrative of Dr. Martin Luther King Jr., as seen in his Birmingham Jail letter, is a perfect example of this. His approach wasn't merely reactive but deeply rooted in a strategy that anticipated and orchestrated the responses it would elicit. This principle of strategic precedence is not just a historical footnote; it's a lesson for anyone aiming to effect substantial change.

People who succeed at change know that strategy is the architect of action. We must think before we act, and the quality of our strategy will determine our outcomes. Without a clear strategy, actions are mere reactions—often emotional, hurried, and ultimately, less effective. They become like arrows shot in the dark, lacking direction and clarity.

Consider the world of chess. The grandmasters of chess plan several moves ahead; each decision builds on the last, always with an eye toward a simple goal. Their victories are the result of deliberate, strategic thinking. They aren't left up to chance. In activism, business, or politics, the leaders who stand out think like chess masters.

Historical examples are everywhere. Mahatma Gandhi's campaign for India's independence from British rule was built on a strategic framework that included nonviolent resistance and civil disobedience. Gandhi's actions were not spontaneous. Each campaign was a carefully planned exercise designed to achieve specific objectives and build toward a larger goal. His strategic acumen ensured that each action taken was a step towards independence, and it worked. In 1947, India became an independent nation.

Strategy is
the architect
of action.

In the business world, few examples are as compelling as Apple Inc. during Steve Jobs' leadership. On his return to Apple, he made a series of strategic decisions that completely changed the company. Each product launch was carefully planned to ensure the company met market demands.

The importance of strategy is not confined to historical figures or corporate giants; it is equally critical in everyday leadership and management. For instance, a manager in a corporate setting must think strategically to meet the company's short-term and long-term objectives. That involves constant consideration, anticipating market changes, understanding competitor moves, and aligning the team's efforts with the company's mission. The absence of such strategic thinking can lead to missed opportunities and operational inefficiencies.

Of course, the success of any strategy hinges on its execution. The strategy must be well thought out, but it must also be frequently adjusted to the realities on the ground. King demonstrated this adaptability exceptionally well. He was flexible and responsive to the shifting dynamics of the civil rights struggle while remaining steadfast in his commitment to the vision.

Putting strategy before action can help us live meaningful and impactful lives, and we will expand on this concept in the next chapter. It requires foresight, patience, and a willingness to adapt, but the efforts are worth it. By embracing this approach, we can navigate complex challenges, marshal resources effectively, and achieve our goals.

Martin Luther King Jr. and other exceptional leaders provide rich examples of what it means to be strategic. They show us that the most enduring changes rely on strategy and activity, but strategy comes first. If we want to make the subtle shifts that will move us forward in a positive direction, we must think strategically and then act—not the other way around.

The perils of premature action

In business, action is often equated with progress, but this assumption can be misleading. Driven by the necessity to achieve results, many develop a bias for action that ultimately proves counterproductive. Cheryl, a chief marketing officer at a rapidly growing startup, was the perfect example of this, and her story illustrates the pitfalls that await when action precedes strategy.

Cheryl joined the startup at a crucial time. The company was young and full of potential but needed a coherent marketing strategy. Her bias for action initially seemed like an asset to the firm, and for the first three years, Cheryl's approach yielded impressive results. Marketing campaigns were launched one after another, and Cheryl's team was busy. The company's lack of structured marketing meant any action taken was better than none, and Cheryl thrived in this chaotic environment.

However, as the startup grew quickly, cracks started to show up in Cheryl's approach. As the company tripled in size, the executives began to question the role that marketing played in the growth. The executive team looked at the marketing department's contributions more critically and didn't like what they saw. They realized that many of Cheryl's recommendations were flippant, and they questioned the rationale behind the campaigns she tried to justify. Without a strategic framework, her decisions appeared arbitrary, rooted more in instinct than insight.

The turning point came during a routine evaluation where it became evident that Cheryl needed a clear marketing strategy. When I was brought in to consult, one of my first questions to her was about her strategic plan. Her response was telling—there was none. She admitted to a lack of justification for her team's activities and acknowledged that she liked to shoot from the hip and go with her gut. Her addiction to action had led her to chase shiny new tactics without considering their long-term impact or alignment with the company's goals.

This realization was crucial, and Cheryl had a choice to make. Either adapt by developing a strategic mindset or continue her current path and face the consequences. Unfortunately, Cheryl decided against change, fought tooth and nail against the advice of others, and insisted on operating without a strategy. Eventually, she was forced to move on as the company went in a different direction. Because she couldn't update her assumptions about the importance of strategic thinking, she had to find another job that better matched her capabilities.

After Cheryl left and a new chief marketing officer took over, the full scope of the previous mismanagement came into focus. The marketing initiatives, largely ineffective, hadn't justified their costs, and the ROI was disappointing. Furthermore, the marketing team expressed how disillusioned and tired they were and thanked the CEO for making the change. Cheryl's lack of strategic acumen drained the business's financial resources and eroded team morale and productivity. The new CMO had a significant hole to dig the team out of but did so successfully because she focused on strategy first and action second.

Cheryl's story is a stark reminder that the rush to act without strategic grounding is not just a pitfall for corporate leaders but a universal hazard that can trip up any of us. Her story underscores a truth applicable to all walks of life and leadership: action without strategy can lead to short-term triumphs that fail to stand the test of time. Strategy is a vital navigational tool, steering us in a direction that aligns with what matters most.

Understanding strategy

To avoid missteps like Cheryl's, we need to think about strategic implications before leaping into action. In our fast-paced world, where immediate gratification often trumps thorough planning, slowing down might seem counterproductive. However, the clarity and foresight that a well-crafted strategy provides are invaluable. They transform actions from mere reactions to proactive steps that build towards a well-defined and attainable future.

Putting strategy first ensures that our initiatives are executed effectively and carry profound and lasting effects. This shift from spontaneous to strategic action is critical for anyone seeking to make a significant impact. Whether you're leading a startup, managing a team, or navigating personal goals, a thoughtfully devised strategy isn't just beneficial—it's crucial. A solid strategy is a reliable ally when decisions have far-reaching consequences.

But what does a solid strategy look like, and what exactly is strategy? Many people struggle with developing a strategic approach because they do not fully understand what strategy entails. To clarify this, let's turn to Michael Porter, who has done extensive academic work on the concept. Porter defines strategy as "deliberately choosing a different set of activities to deliver unique

Shift from spontaneous to strategic action.

value."³ This definition highlights the importance of differentiation and uniqueness in strategic choices. Companies and individuals can distinguish themselves from competitors by selecting a unique set of activities, thus creating a competitive advantage.

Building on Porter's idea, Roger Martin, another brilliant thinker in the management field, offers another core concept. I've talked about his idea of integrative thinking in an earlier chapter, which is all about balancing conflicting ideas to develop a better solution than either option alone. But in his book with A. G. Lafley, *Playing to Win: How Strategy Really Works*, Martin gets into the nuts and bolts of strategy.⁴ He says it boils down to choosing where to compete and how to win. It's like choosing your battlefield and planning the best way to conquer it.

Martin's take on strategy helps us see it as a couple of clear choices. Deciding where to play and how to win are critical choices we must continuously make. It's about being selective, not just running with every opportunity that comes your way. This selectiveness is crucial because it helps you focus your energy and resources on what will help you stand out and succeed.

In practical terms, being strategic means knowing your strengths and weaknesses and having a good read on the competition. What are they good at? Where do they falter? Knowing this helps you find your niche—where you can excel. Then, it's about continuously adjusting your approach as things change around you, whether it's new competition, changing customer preferences, or other market shifts.

So, strategy isn't just a fancy business plan; it's about making thoughtful choices, understanding your unique value, and always being ready to adapt. Think of it as playing chess, not checkers. You need to think several moves ahead, anticipate your opponent's moves, and adjust yours along the way. This combination of questioning, understanding, and selecting helps you make a lasting impact, no matter the area you're working in.

Pause and ponder

It's so easy to get caught up in the rush to act, to solve problems immediately, or to seize fleeting opportunities when we have a bias toward action. However, success requires a more reflective approach, and I always tell my clients to pause and ponder before making decisions. As an executive coach, I've witnessed firsthand how powerful pausing can be. When we slow things down and take a few minutes to think, we move away from the impulse to act and move toward our inner wisdom.

Starting with strategy means consciously choosing to step back and evaluate the broader implications of our actions. In an environment where leaders constantly juggle competing priorities and scarce time, making this pause a routine practice is challenging. The pressure to deliver immediate results can overshadow the need for thoughtful planning and drive us directly into action. However, this approach often leads to short-sighted decisions that may solve immediate issues but fail to address the underlying challenges that really hold us back. That is why I'm ending this chapter with seven practices that will help you think strategically when the impulse to act surfaces. Committing to these practices ensures that your actions are deliberate, considered, and aligned with a vision of sustained growth and success in today's complex, fast-paced environment.

REFLECT BEFORE YOU ACT

We often feel pressure to make decisions quickly to maintain momentum or meet external expectations. However, taking a step back to reflect can prevent costly errors and misalignments. Begin by defining clear objectives and identifying potential obstacles. Consider various scenarios and their possible impacts. This reflection period doesn't have to be long, but it should be integral to your decision-making process. It allows you to assess the strategic value of each action thoroughly.

One of my clients, Sarah, learned this the hard way. She rushed a product launch without fully considering the market's readiness, resulting in significant financial loss for her company. After working together, Sarah learned to relax her bias toward action. Now, whenever she is excited about an idea, she takes time to define her objectives and get clear about the outcomes she is trying to achieve. She imagines various scenarios and their impacts and makes better decisions as a result.

GATHER DIVERSE PERSPECTIVES

No single person has all the answers. You can gain a broader perspective on potential strategies by involving individuals in conversations and queries. When you encourage open discussions with others, you expand your options and reduce risk. This collaborative approach enhances your strategy and promotes a sense of shared ownership and teamwork. It is how movements are made.

When Martin Luther King Jr. sat down to write his letter, the words that flowed from within him were a culmination of conversations he had with others as they struggled with the daily injustices and indignities faced by African Americans. His strategy wasn't just a perspective he created alone. It resulted from thousands of conversations with other leading thinkers at the time. The strategy he articulated in the Letter from a Birmingham Jail was informed by diverse perspectives.

USE DATA TO GUIDE DECISIONS

In today's data-driven world, relying on gut feeling alone is insufficient. Use data to make informed decisions about the strategies you plan to employ. Analyze historical data, market trends, and competitive analyses to forecast potential outcomes. Data helps justify strategic decisions and provides a benchmark against which you can measure success.

One of Steve Jobs' first strategic moves was dramatically simplifying Apple's product line. Many believed this move was simply a personal preference aligned with Jobs' desire for simplicity. They presented the move as an example of the sharp focus essential to effective leadership, but there is more to the story. A mountain of data pointed toward the need for a new direction. Apple had lost $1.04 billion in 1997, and the data suggested that 70% of the product line was redundant, Apple's market share was declining, and public perception of the company was plummeting.[5] Steve Jobs' decision to dramatically reduce the product line wasn't made on gut instinct alone. He used data to guide that decision.

PRIORITIZE LONG-TERM RESULTS OVER SHORT-TERM WINS

While seeking quick wins is tempting, sustainable success requires a long-term view. Set goals that align with your overall vision and work backward to establish steps to achieve these objectives. This might mean passing up on immediate opportunities that don't align with your long-term strategy.

A profound illustration of this principle can be seen in the life of Nelson Mandela. After spending twenty-seven years in prison, Nelson Mandela emerged not with a message of retribution but with one of reconciliation and a vision for a unified South Africa. This vision required him to prioritize long-term peace and equality over the short-term gains of punitive justice against the apartheid regime. Mandela's choice to engage in negotiations with the very individuals who had enforced apartheid was a strategic decision aimed at the larger goal of national stability and integration rather than immediate satisfaction.

SCHEDULE REGULAR STRATEGY REVIEWS

The landscape is constantly evolving, and so should your strategy. Schedule regular review sessions to evaluate the effectiveness of your methods. This approach is crucial for adapting to changes in the market or your internal operations. Adjustments may be necessary, but they should always be made with strategic intent.

One way to think about this is to imagine you are a coach of an athletic team. The sport could be soccer, football, basketball, or something similar. If your team was losing, would you stick to your original strategy or change it up? You might call a timeout to recalibrate or use a halftime break to change your approach entirely.

The same is true in life or leadership. Similar to how a coach adjusts their strategies based on the game's progress, it would be best to remain flexible and responsive to your environment. Regular pauses to evaluate your strategy allow you to pivot or alter your approaches based on feedback and results. This agility is critical to staying competitive and relevant.

EDUCATE YOUR TEAM ON STRATEGIC CHOICES

For a strategy to be effective, everyone involved needs to understand what they are doing and why they are doing it. They also need to appreciate the strategies that guide the team's actions. Invest time in teaching your team about the strategic importance of their roles and the organization's broader objectives. This understanding can motivate employees to align their daily tasks with strategic goals.

A great example of the power of strategic education can be seen in the actions of Martin Luther King Jr. and other leaders during the civil rights movement. King understood that for their nonviolent protests to be effective, every participant needed to be deeply aligned with the strategy and principles behind their actions. In his Letter from a Birmingham Jail, King detailed how the movement prepared for direct action: "We were not unmindful of the difficulties involved. So, we decided to go through a process of self-purification. We started having workshops on nonviolence and repeatedly asked ourselves the questions, 'Are you able to accept blows without retaliating?' and 'Are you able to endure the ordeals of jail?'" These training sessions were crucial in ensuring that demonstrators were physically prepared and mentally and emotionally committed to the strategic approach of nonviolence.

This thorough education on the strategy and its underlying principles empowered each participant to act consistently and effectively despite the personal risks. The workshops helped to forge a unified front, where everyone's actions were synchronized with the collective strategy, maximizing the impact of their efforts and the movement as a whole. Just as King and his fellow leaders educated their teams on the strategic importance of their roles within the civil rights movement, modern leaders must also ensure their teams understand and are committed to the strategies that guide their collective efforts.

COMMIT TO CONTINUOUS LEARNING

Strategic acumen is not a static skill—it develops with experience and continuous learning. Commit yourself to constantly questioning and learning from the strategies you employ. Ensure your strategies are working, and don't be afraid to try new approaches. Our habits and biases can keep us from recognizing when our strategies are off, and we need to be willing to push ourselves outside of our comfort zones.

Several years ago, one of my clients, Josh, learned a hard lesson about leadership. He had always used a forceful and direct approach, believing that openly criticizing underperformance was the best way to motivate his team. This method seemed practical until one day, during a high-stress meeting, he pushed a team member to the point of tears. This incident was a turning point for Josh. It starkly revealed how his approach was hurting people and damaging his relationships.

Realizing the need for change, Josh sought guidance to reevaluate his leadership style. We identified and codified the strategy driving his behavior through our coaching sessions. Josh began to see how his subconscious strategies adversely affected his team's performance and perception of him. Armed with this insight, he was motivated to adopt a new strategy focused on constructive feedback and support rather than criticism.

The shift in Josh's approach had a transformative impact on his team and was an excellent example of how continuous learning helps us grow. By breaking down the strategy driving his behavior, Josh was able to design a much more effective new strategy. Moreover, he modeled flexibility and creative leadership by showing his team that change is possible.

Chapter Summary

- In any movement, the sequence of actions can mean the difference between profound success and disheartening failure.
- Effective change agents understand that strategy is the architect of action. It shapes the path, defines the approach, and ensures that every step taken is purposeful and impactful.
- If we want to make the subtle shifts that will move us forward in a positive direction, we must think strategically and then act—not the other way around.
- Starting with strategy means consciously choosing to step back and evaluate the broader implications of our actions.
- In our fast-paced world, it's easy to get caught up in the rush to act, solve problems immediately, or seize fleeting opportunities. However, excellence requires a more reflective approach that emphasizes pausing and pondering before making decisions.
- Commit to seven practices when you pause to ensure your actions are deliberate, considered, and aligned with a vision promoting sustained growth and success in today's complex, fast-paced environment.

EIGHT

Calibrate: Align your Actions

"Efficiency is doing things right; effectiveness is doing the right things."
~ Peter Drucker

Planning prevents poor performance, right? Well, not so fast. While the adage suggests that well-laid plans lead to success, reality often tells a different story. Enter the concept of the planning fallacy, a term coined by cognitive psychologists Daniel Kahneman and Amos Tversky.[1] This fallacy highlights our tendency to underestimate the time, costs, and risks of future actions, while simultaneously overestimating the benefits. In essence, we are terrible planners. We are wired to be overly optimistic about our plans, often leading to less-than-stellar outcomes.

Many of us know this to be true, especially those facing leadership trials. Dwight D. Eisenhower captured it best when he said, "In preparing for battle, I have always found that plans are useless, but planning is indispensable."² This insight aligns with what many intuitively feel: planning has value, but plans are rarely worth the paper they are written on. Even the great philosopher and former heavyweight champion Mike Tyson knew this was true. He once said, "Everyone has a plan until they get punched in the face," and he was right.³ Our plans often falter under pressure despite how good they make us feel.

In the previous chapter, we established the importance of prioritizing strategy over action. We learned that a sound strategy sets a clear direction and provides a foundation for our actions. We also learned that examining and codifying our strategies can help us confidently act. But strategy is only a piece of the puzzle.

In this chapter, I want you to consider another vital concept that will help you shift your actions: strategy will only get us so far if we do not continuously calibrate that strategy and the actions that go along with it. As we go out into the real world to implement our strategy, we must remain agile, adjusting our course in response to new information and changing conditions. This ongoing calibration process ensures that our strategies remain relevant and that our actions are aligned.

The problem with plans

When I was fresh out of graduate school, I was selected to lead a significant change management and training program in the federal government. The agency I was consulting with had just redesigned its case management system, and everyone in the chief information officer's office was brimming with enthusiasm. This project, which had been delayed for five years and was millions of dollars over

Strategy will only get us so far.

budget, was finally about to cross the finish line, and the newly appointed CIO wanted a quick win.

As I built my team and started to evaluate the software and business processes, I realized we had a problem. The more we dove into the new system, the more obvious it became that the software wasn't ready for prime time. Despite all the planning, time, and money thrown into it, it was a mess. It was hard to use and not at all user-friendly. Simple tasks that used to take twenty seconds were now taking two minutes to complete, and it was clear that the software was the bottleneck. The software had been developed without the user experience in mind, and the rollout was headed for disaster.

Breaking the news to the CIO was one of the toughest professional things I have ever had to do, but it was necessary. The software couldn't go out like this. As a worst-case scenario, the employees who had to use the software would revolt. Even if I could wave a magic wand and convince them it would all be okay, the software would negatively affect the organization's productivity.

I made my case as best as I could, but the CIO wasn't having it. He had come into this organization with a mandate to get this software out the door and wouldn't accept any further delays. "We have a plan, and we are sticking to it," he told me, "The software will be released according to the plan." He scolded me for pushing back and told me I better get on board. He wanted me to know that he was committed to the plan, and he wanted me to do the same.

Within days of the software's release, the consequences started rolling in. Complaints poured in from the field, and the CIO was called to the carpet. Productivity decreased significantly, and the higher-ups weren't happy with the CIO. Even they could see that he was too married to the plan and one-dimensional in his thinking. They tried to set him straight, but he remained stubborn. He wouldn't deviate from the plan.

Within one year of the software's release, he was looking for a new job, but the damage was done. The backlog of work had grown exponentially, and productivity didn't recover for years. The organization had to invest in new leadership, software, and other damage control measures.

It turns out that sticking to the plan wasn't the best strategy. In fact, planning was mistaken for strategy, and the organization paid the price. By falling in love with the plan, failing to question the plan, and assuming that the project's problems were merely problems of execution, the CIO did a disservice to the agency. His blind trust in the plan resulted in a lot of damage, and he later admitted that he was too focused on doing things right rather than doing the right thing.

At its essence, this is the problem with plans. Too many of us follow them blindly. In a complex, fast-moving, and ever-changing world, we look to plans to ease our minds and give us solid ground to stand on. When someone steps up and confidently provides us with a plan, we often buy in because of the planner's confidence rather than the plan's merits. Unfortunately, many plans are like a house of cards—fragile and prone to collapse at the slightest disruption. They might appear stable but lack the flexibility and resilience to adapt to unexpected changes and challenges.

Continuous calibration creates a stellar performance.

What's the alternative

If we can't rely on plans, what can we rely on? It's a big question for anyone trying to navigate an unpredictable world. When the structured frameworks we so carefully designed begin to crumble under the weight of real-world complexities, it's not our plans but the people behind the plans who become our most reliable resource. It turns out that success doesn't come from crafting the perfect plan—it comes from harnessing the gifts and talents of the people who execute these plans.

Consider the metaphor of a symphony orchestra. In a symphony, each musician brings a unique skill set to the stage. The strings, brass, and percussionists all have different parts to play, but their collective effort creates the music. Each musician is asked to follow a plan, but they also pay attention to the conductor to make subtle adjustments along the way. This example of continuous calibration creates a stellar performance, and we can learn a lot from the symphony.

In organizations, success results from diverse talents and efforts converging toward a common goal. Just as a conductor guides an orchestra, aligning each musician's contributions to the overall performance, a business leader must align the efforts of their team members to execute projects successfully. The team and the leader must calibrate their actions to optimize performance.

Every team member is like a musician in an orchestra. They have specific roles, responsibilities, and expertise that they bring to the table. For example, the marketing expert crafts compelling narratives around the product, the salesperson builds relationships and closes deals, and the customer service representative ensures client satisfaction. Everyone plays a critical role in the symphony of business, and performances are rarely isolated. They are interdependent, and they must work together to reach their objectives.

Leaders are at their best when they cultivate this symphony of talents. They must acknowledge diverse skills and create an environment where these skills can emerge and combine. They often have to ditch the predetermined plan and calibrate actions to meet pressing needs. They must respond to the realities on the ground, adjust their tactics, deal with challenges, encourage change, and allow for improvisation and adaptation when necessary.

Every successful project is the culmination of many efforts. For instance, launching a new product isn't just a victory for the product development team but a triumph of collaboration across various departments. Market research influences design decisions, customer feedback informs adjustments, and sales strategies evolve based on real-time sales. This interconnectedness transforms individual efforts into collective achievements.

So, rigid plans are not the backbone of success. The better support structure is made up of the individuals who make up your team. When we recognize this and work to align diverse talents, we bring out the best in people and produce the best outcomes. But how can we foster this harmonious interaction? How do we ensure that the individual performances blend into a symphony we want to be a part of? We do so by focusing on alignment.

Agonizing over alignment

The importance of alignment cannot be overstated. It directly impacts every aspect of an organization's operations. From productivity and efficiency to employee satisfaction and morale, alignment ensures everyone moves in the same direction. It fosters a sense of unity and purpose, and it reduces conflicts and misunderstandings. Unfortunately, achieving alignment is easier said than done.

Consider the findings from a study in the Harvard Business Review article, *Is Your Company as Strategically Aligned as You Think It Is?*[4] The article highlights a common but critical misconception within many organizations—people often think we have alignment when we don't. In the article, the authors share a story about a CEO who, fresh from a strategy retreat, feels confident that everyone is completely aligned with the company's strategy. However, the researchers discover a different story. While employees reported 82% aligned with the company's strategies, a deeper look showed actual alignment was a dismal 23%. That's a big reality check: many of us think we're on the same page when we're not even reading the same book.

This disconnect illustrates an important issue. Despite our best intentions, achieving alignment is challenging, and many of our efforts don't work. Take mission statements, for example. Everyone knows a clear mission should guide organizations, so we spend time writing and communicating about them. Unfortunately, despite all our efforts, very few can articulate that mission. Studies show that up to 61% of employees do not know their company's mission statement, and of the ones who do, 57% are not motivated by it.

Dismal statistics also exist when we look at alignment around organizational values. Only 26% of U.S. employees strongly agree that their company consistently delivers on its promises, and only 27% strongly agree that they believe in their company's values.[5] To make matters worse, merely 23% of U.S. employees strongly agree that they can apply their organization's values to their work. These figures suggest a significant disconnect between stated values and practical application for most employees.

The problem also exists at a more tactical level. 44% of projects fail due to a lack of alignment between business and project objectives.[6] Another study of 124 organizations revealed that only 28% of executives and middle managers responsible for executing strategy could list three of their company's strategic priorities.[7] If executives and middle managers aren't aligned around priorities, how is anyone supposed to implement them? Alignment is a problem across the board.

Achieving alignment

Achieving alignment requires fundamental shifts in how we operate, but these shifts don't have to be dramatic. History shows us that great leaders achieved greatness through subtle acts of alignment.

We see this in the stories of Martin Luther King Jr., Winston Churchill, Mahatma Gandhi, and Michael J. Fox. It's easy to attribute their success to the traits they possessed or the bold actions they took. Yes, they stood courageously against external pressures, faced massive challenges, and were brilliant orators who inspired crowds. They were outstanding individuals, and many of their actions were seismic. However, attributing their success to the apparent factors alone overlooks the subtle actions that made a difference.

Martin Luther King Jr. was arrested thirty times during his thirteen years as a civil rights leader. Can you imagine the persistence and fortitude he had to have to continue his fight for civil rights? His ability to align people with the vision of equality and justice was not just through his powerful speeches. His relentless commitment to the cause demonstrated that authentic leadership and alignment often come from a place of deep inner strength and unwavering determination.

Winston Churchill often worked eighteen-hour days and endured a barrage of London bombings as he led England during WWII. Sure, several of those hours were in his bedroom, but don't you think he was persistent and had to demonstrate great endurance during those times? Churchill's alignment with his country's fight for survival came from his relentless work ethic and ability to keep the British unified and motivated, even in the darkest hours.

Similarly, Mahatma Gandhi's success in leading India to independence was not just about his nonviolent resistance but also his incredible patience and ability to align millions with peaceful protest. Gandhi's subtle yet powerful acts of humility and unwavering patience created a cohesive and resilient movement.

After being diagnosed with Parkinson's disease, Michael J. Fox did not just rely on his fame to drive his advocacy for research. His enduring optimism, passion for the cause, and continuous effort to engage others in his foundation's mission have created a strong alignment among researchers, donors, and the public, pushing the boundaries of what can be achieved.

These leaders achieved alignment through unwavering commitment and subtle shifts in action. History books often highlight a leader's traits, grand gestures, and dramatic moments, but they frequently miss the nuances and details that made these leaders great. Their small, consistent actions—King's countless local meetings, Churchill's constant wordsmithing before communicating with the British people, Gandhi's daily spinning of the charkha, and Fox's ongoing engagement with the Parkinson's community—created lasting alignment.

These subtle and nuanced actions were the driving force behind their success. They understood that alignment wasn't achieved through a single grand gesture but through continuous, dedicated effort. They didn't just set a vision; they lived it daily through their actions. They consistently brought people along, one subtle shift at a time.

Continuous calibration

When you look closely at what produces alignment, you realize it is an ongoing effort. Alignment doesn't come from a strategic plan, a leadership offsite, a staff retreat, or an annual goal-setting session. It doesn't materialize after monthly or weekly staff meetings or one-on-one progress reviews. It doesn't even come from combining these episodic events. Alignment is the result of something much more subtle.

Alignment comes from a commitment to continuous calibration—a nuanced art where constant, minor adjustments and refinements keep everyone moving in the same direction. This art form differs significantly from most people's traditional, episodic approach when creating alignment. Instead of being a one-time event or a series of sporadic check-ins, it is a dynamic, ongoing process. Remember how we talked about steering a car on a long stretch of highway? If you take your hands off the wheel and stop paying attention, the car will gradually drift off course and end up where you'll have to move the steering wheel to correct your mistake dramatically. To avoid this, we constantly make subtle shifts to keep the car in the lane.

Continuous calibration works in much the same way. It requires constant, minor adjustments to ensure everyone remains aligned with the desired outcomes. By regularly assessing and fine-tuning our approach, we can address any misalignments early on. There are four steps you can take to do this efficiently.

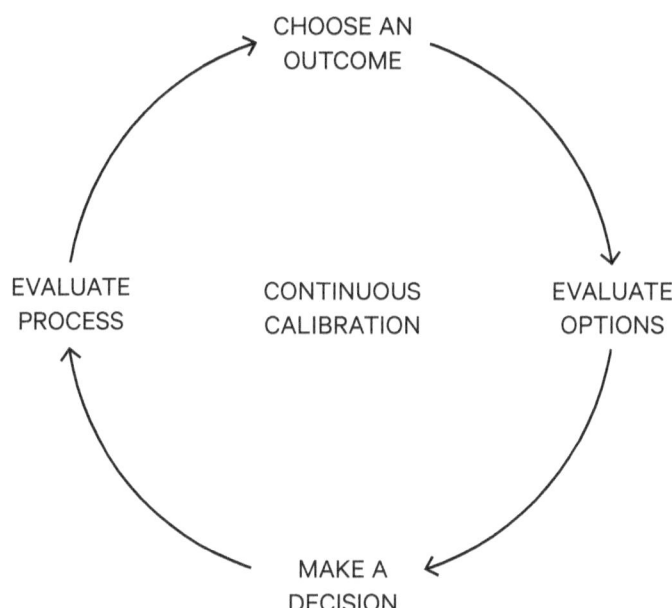

CHOOSE AN OUTCOME

The first step in continuous calibration is to choose a clear, specific outcome. This involves defining success and ensuring that everyone understands what it looks like. The outcome must be aligned with the overarching strategy and vision. Questions to ask at this stage include: What are we trying to achieve? How does this outcome align with our strategic goals? What will success look like?

I worked with a tech startup that wanted to improve customer satisfaction. The customer success manager gathered the team and defined the desired outcome: to increase customer satisfaction scores by 15% over six months. This clear, specific outcome provided the team with a target to aim for and clarified what success looked like. It also offered a way to measure success and gave everyone a scoreboard to pay attention to. The initiative was a huge success, achieving a 15% increase and surpassing it. The improved satisfaction scores led to higher customer retention, increased word-of-mouth referrals, and a stronger overall reputation in the market.

That is the power of clearly stating an outcome. A team becomes more focused and driven when it has a well-defined target. Clear outcomes align everyone's efforts toward a common goal and create a sense of unity and purpose in a team. Additionally, having a specific outcome allows for better progress tracking and makes it easier to identify areas that need adjustment.

EVALUATE OPTIONS

Once the outcome is chosen, we must evaluate options to achieve it. That involves brainstorming, gathering data, and considering the actions we should take. It is crucial to put all options on the table and weigh the pros and cons of each, but we mustn't get stuck in analysis paralysis. Too often, teams either jump into action too quickly or take too long considering options. Either extreme leads to wasted effort or misplaced action and keeps us from reaching our goals.

To find the right balance, ask: What are our options for achieving this outcome? What options work best? What are the potential benefits and risks of each option? By considering these questions quickly and efficiently, we can navigate the decision-making

Clear outcomes align everyone's efforts.

process without getting bogged down. We can also remain agile and responsive as we search for a pragmatic pathway forward.

The tech startup I worked with modeled this perfectly. They evaluated several options for improving customer satisfaction, devised many ideas, evaluated each idea quickly, and avoided analysis paralysis. They didn't act too soon, and they also didn't get lost in the process. The customer success manager also did something brilliant. She involved the entire team in the evaluation process, encouraged open discussions, and welcomed diverse perspectives. This approach ensured that all potential options were thoroughly considered, and the team felt a sense of ownership over the chosen actions.

MAKE A DECISION

After evaluating your options, it is time to decide. You must stop evaluating options and make a choice. The Roman philosopher Cicero once said, "More is lost by indecision than wrong decision. Indecision is the thief of opportunity. It will steal you blind." If we want to be successful, we must make the best decisions with the information we have. Indecision isn't an option when we want to get everyone acting in concert.

At this stage in the game, we don't want to ask questions; we want to answer them. Your key priorities are choosing what actions to take, who will do what, by when, and who needs to know this decision. Making a timely and decisive choice will propel the team forward and safeguard against missed opportunities.

Continuing with the tech startup example, I will never forget how decisive the customer experience manager was when she made her decision. Even though she and the team considered many possible actions, she quickly and decisively chose a path forward and communicated it to the team. She was honest with them about the methods she used to decide and made a strong case for the path forward. She also expressed her commitment and asked others to do the same.

Despite the strong case for her approach, some team members disagreed with her decision. They believed other options would be more effective, and some felt the decision would harm them. Recognizing their concerns, my client took the time to acknowledge their perspectives and express genuine appreciation for their contributions. She listened to their concerns, explained her rationale clearly, and emphasized that the decision was about selecting the best option from many "right" options. This framing helped the team feel valued and validated, even if their preferred option wasn't selected.

Once the decision was made, she explained it clearly and confidently. She laid out the plan decisively, ensuring everyone understood their roles and responsibilities. There was no wavering; her resolve inspired the team to move forward with conviction. This clear communication and steadfast leadership were crucial in maintaining alignment and momentum as the team embarked on the new training program.

EVALUATE PROGRESS

The final step in the continuous calibration process is regularly checking progress. It involves monitoring our implementation, gathering feedback, and making necessary adjustments. It is crucial to keep the lines of communication open and ensure everyone is aware of the progress. Questions to ask at this stage include: Are we progressing toward our outcome? What feedback are we receiving? What adjustments do we need to make?

In the tech startup example, my client scheduled regular check-ins to review the progress of the customer service training program. The team gathered feedback from customer service representatives and customers, identified areas for improvement, and made necessary adjustments to the program. This ongoing process of checking progress and making adjustments ensures that the team stays aligned with their goal of improving customer satisfaction. For example, if customer feedback indicates that response times are too slow, the team might hire additional support staff or implement new software to streamline customer interactions.

Organizations can create a continuous loop of alignment and adjustment by following this framework of choosing an outcome, evaluating options, making a decision, and checking on progress. This approach fosters a culture of agility, clarity, accessibility, and accountability, enabling organizations to remain resilient, adaptable, and focused on their goals, even in constant change and uncertainty.

Chapter Summary

- Shifting our actions requires us to engage in continuous calibration.
- The planning fallacy suggests that we are terrible planners. We are wired to be overly optimistic about our plans, often leading to less-than-stellar outcomes.
- Don't follow plans mindlessly. Plans are often like a house of cards—fragile and prone to collapse at the slightest disruption.
- Strategy is essential, but it will only get us so far. Stellar results occur when winning actions are aligned with a winning strategy.
- Alignment with a strategy is just as important as the strategy itself. Alignment comes from a commitment to continuous calibration, a nuanced art in which constant, small adjustments and refinements keep everyone moving in the same direction.
- Alignment requires subtle adjustments to ensure everyone remains aligned with the desired outcomes. By regularly assessing and fine-tuning our actions, we can address any misalignments early on.

NINE

Navigate: Finding the Sweet Spot

"To go beyond is as wrong as to fall short."
~ Confucius

Before I started my business, I had the privilege of leading a large team in the federal government. This experience was both challenging and rewarding, and it gave me a firsthand look at what it takes to lead a diverse team in a bureaucratic organization. I learned a lot through the experience, but the real learning came from a moment of self-reflection after completing a 360-degree review in an executive development program. What I discovered was more important than I could have ever anticipated. It set the stage for one of the most significant changes in my approach to leadership and life.

At the time, I was in my mid-30s and confident in my leadership abilities. I was part of a strong executive leadership team, and my division performed well. My peers and I were satisfied that we were meeting most of our objectives with high efficiency and teamwork, and our customers seemed to agree. When the opportunity for a 360° review came up, I welcomed it, expecting affirmations of my leadership style and a few pointers on areas for improvement.

The initial feedback was great. People saw me as an effective leader, and I scored at the 92nd percentile on the instrument's leadership effectiveness dimension. It was also nice to see that my raters shared positive comments about my ability to build relationships, achieve results, and think strategically and systematically. But as I dove deeper into the report, I was confronted with feedback that hit me right between the eyes.

The comments said it all. One person wrote, "Matt can come across as arrogant." Another said, "Matt needs to realize that he is a bit too critical and isn't always right." And the final nail in the coffin, "Matt should know that pointing out what is wrong doesn't help others do what is right." Ouch! The feedback was a tough pill to swallow.

While I thought my approach was necessary for our success, it created an unintended barrier between myself and the team. To make matters worse, I was completely unaware that my behavior was having this effect on others. The way I was showing up was a complete blind spot. During the debrief with my coach, I launched into a long-winded explanation of why others saw me this way.

I told him I was aware of my critical nature and explained that I disliked that part of me. I suggested that being critical was just part of who I was and argued that the job required it of me. As a leader, I was expected to have high standards and hold others accountable. I confidently analyzed my critical nature out loud and tried to prove that I thoroughly understood it, but the more I spoke, the more I realized I didn't know what the hell I was talking about. This became even more evident when my coach stopped me mid-sentence.

"Matt, I have to be honest. It sounds like you are feeling a bit defensive, but let me ask you something. Do you think it's possible to maintain high standards without being perceived as overly critical or arrogant?" His question caught me off guard and sliced through my defensive monologue like a knife through butter. I didn't know what to say, so I just sat there, feeling like an idiot.

He continued, asking if it was okay for him to challenge me. I agreed, and he shared how I had shown up with him. He told me that the way I was behaving at this very moment felt very defensive, critical, and arrogant. He provided a few specific examples and helped me see that the justifications I was making, the explanations I was giving, and the words I was using reinforced the feedback others provided. He asked if this was how I typically responded to information that made me uncomfortable and suggested that I take a long, hard look at my reactive nature. "If you are so aware of your critical nature and don't like that about yourself, why do you keep acting that way?" he asked. Looking at him like a deer staring in headlights, I realized that in my rush to prove that I had a handle on my results, I hadn't considered that my reaction was demonstrating the same behaviors that others deemed critical and arrogant.

A critical distinction

Discovering that others felt this way about me felt like a slap in the face. I remember sitting in that debrief and feeling a flood of emotions. I was frustrated, hurt, confused, and, honestly, a bit angry. My position was challenging enough without confronting these uncomfortable truths about myself. I had poured my heart and soul into my work, aiming to push my team to achieve excellence, and here I was, facing feedback that, quite frankly, was alarming.

Recognizing that my leadership style had this effect on people wasn't what I wanted to hear. I wanted to be a good leader others appreciated and admired. However, it forced me to question my methods and the essence of my leadership approach. How could I be a great leader without having this effect on people? This question loomed large as I left the debrief, but it began a profound and necessary evolution toward understanding and change.

When I met with my coach a week later, he asked me how I felt about the feedback. I told him I was feeling down and explained that I didn't want to be perceived as critical or arrogant. I shared that I had come to accept the feedback, but I didn't know what to do about it. Thankfully, he knew exactly what to say. "You know, Matt, what one person calls critical, another calls discerning." He asked, "What would it be like to show up as discerning rather than critical?"

At first, I didn't have an answer to his question. To be honest, I wasn't quite sure what he was getting at. But as we continued the conversation, it began to click. He explained that discernment and criticism are like two sides of the same coin. Both come from the same positive intention—a desire to achieve excellence and ensure the team is performing at its best—but criticism pursues the intention aggressively and antagonistically. In contrast, discernment pursues it deliberately and diplomatically.

He went on to explain that several behaviors and traits operate similarly. There is often a fine line between behaviors perceived as positive and those perceived as negative. Take being assertive, for example. Many of us want our leaders to be assertive until we don't. We want them to be confident, clear, and a bit forceful when necessary, but we want them to turn it off when assertiveness goes too far and turns into aggression. Independence and isolation also work in much the same way. We love it when people work independently but don't like it much if independence leads to isolation and a lack of collaboration.

The distinction my coach and I explored made me realize something profound. Leaders succeed or fail because of nuance. My coach and I discussed how leadership is paradoxical and requires a deep understanding of when to push and when to pull back. It's about reading the room and adapting to the situation at hand, which becomes even more critical as the complexities of team dynamics and individual personalities come into play. This understanding made me reflect on how my actions, though well-intentioned, often missed the mark. It was clear that I needed to develop a more flexible approach to leadership. One that allowed me to navigate the nuance required to succeed.

We discussed how effective leaders manage this balance almost instinctively. They know when to assert themselves to drive a point home and when to step back and let others lead the way. This delicate balancing act is what sets genuinely respected leaders apart from those who are merely tolerated or, worse, resented by their teams. Leaders who understand and navigate the fine line between constructive and destructive actions perform better than leaders who don't.

Armed with this new perspective, I set out to transform my approach. I focused on being more mindful of my tone and words, ensuring they conveyed support rather than judgment. I tried to listen more than I spoke, which helped me understand the tasks and the emotional undercurrents within the team. This shift didn't happen overnight. It took consistent effort and sometimes felt like rewiring my entire personality. But the results were undeniable. Over time, I noticed a change in how my team interacted with me and each other. The atmosphere improved, and I felt more comfortable and at peace.

Defining moments

Those conversations with my coach changed my life. They helped me realize the effect I was having on others, but more importantly, they helped me identify the source of my discontent. For years, I was dedicated to climbing the corporate ladder. I played the game and did all that I could to be successful by what I thought were society's standards. I worked hard, paid my dues, and looked at growth linearly. However, this approach left me feeling unfulfilled and disconnected.

The 360° assessment made me recognize that my ambition was blinding me. In my relentless pursuit of achievement and excellence, I lost sight of my real goal: to be a good leader with strong relationships with the people around me. I realized that my drive to succeed made me ridged and, in many ways, too focused. The resulting actions often came at the expense of the connections that could have enriched my professional and personal life.

The insights gained through the work with my coach set me on a path that led me to where I am today—happy and successfully connecting with people on a deeper level as a coach, author, and speaker. The insights also evolved and inspired many concepts I share in this book. My coach's ability to challenge my assumptions and guide me toward a more nuanced understanding of my behavior was transformative. It allowed me to see that leadership isn't just about setting high standards and achieving results; it's also about navigating the complex landscape of our behaviors and emotions.

In the decade that followed my 360° review, I've expanded my understanding and conviction around the importance of subtle shifts. I've seen firsthand how small shifts in actions can significantly improve a leader's effectiveness. I've helped hundreds of clients consider how subtle actions affect others and confirmed that success comes from navigating nuance and making subtle shifts.

Despite all that I have learned, I occasionally fall short. The truth is that making subtle shifts requires intention, persistence, and patience. It isn't a quick fix or an easy adjustment; it's an ongoing effort and a commitment to a different way of living.

Every day, we are faced with choices regarding how we show up. We must choose our actions and whether we want to shift those actions. Each interaction, decision, and response allows us to be more mindful and intentional. By examining our actions, questioning them, adjusting them, and experimenting with new actions, we can position ourselves for significant success. However, this will only happen if we realize that every moment in our lives is a defining moment, and at every moment, we can choose what we do and how we show up.

Appreciating awareness

This awareness brings both challenges and opportunities. The challenge lies in the need for continuous self-reflection and adjustment. It requires us to be present and aware, to notice our behaviors and their impact on others. We must be willing to ask ourselves difficult questions: Am I acting out of habit or with

Making subtle shifts is a lifelong process.

intention? Are my actions aligned with my values and goals? How might others perceive my behavior, and is that the effect I want to have?

The opportunity, however, is equally significant. Each moment presents a chance to change positively and align our actions more closely with our true selves and aspirations. By embracing the concept of subtle shifts, we can gradually transform our leadership, our lives, and the lives of those around us. We can make minor, deliberate adjustments leading to profound and lasting impact.

I've come to understand that making subtle shifts is a lifelong process. It isn't something to achieve or a final destination. Instead, it's about continuous growth and improvement. It's about being compassionate with ourselves when we fall short and celebrating the small victories along the way. That means regularly reflecting on our interactions, seeking feedback, and being open to learning and evolving. It means being patient and understanding that change takes time.

As a coach, I strive to help others embrace subtle shifts and observe their actions by encouraging clients to see every moment as a defining moment that isn't filled with pressure but opportunity. I support them in making subtle shifts, being more intentional in their actions, and appreciating the subtle distinctions in our behaviors.

Navigating nuance

Leadership, at its essence, is both an art and a science. It is an exercise in nuance that we all need to master. The difference between a leader who inspires and alienates is the subtle behaviors and actions that influence their results and effectiveness. If they can't master the art of making subtle shifts—like a driver making slight course corrections as they drive down the highway—they will crash and burn.

Nowhere is this more evident than in our use of language. The choice of words can build bridges or create barriers. For instance, a leader discussing team performance might intend to motivate by saying, "We need to seriously step up our game". But the choice of "seriously" and "step up" might come across as more of a reprimand than encouragement, especially if the tone and context aren't carefully managed. Such words can motivate one person and demotivate another, and that is what makes communication so hard.

Similarly, non-verbal communication plays a crucial role. For example, a leader's posture can send strong signals about their openness and approachability. Crossed arms, a furrowed brow, or a consistently averted gaze—though subtle and subconscious—can be perceived as unapproachable or disinterested. These signals can stifle open communication within the team, as members may feel the leader is uninterested in dialogue or feedback.

Timing is another critical aspect where nuance matters greatly. Consider a leader who extends discussions or arguments beyond a productive limit. Arguing a point for a minute or two longer than necessary might not seem like much, but it can be enough to shift a team's mood from cooperative to resistant. It can transform a healthy debate into a stressful conflict, shifting the focus from resolving the issue to winning the argument.

Leaders often encounter situations where their reactions or lack of awareness can lead to unintended consequences. In high-stress situations, a leader might speak more abruptly or react more sharply than intended. Without realizing it, this subtle shift in delivery can alarm team members or cause undue stress, making the environment feel more crisis-driven than it is.

Another subtle yet common misstep occurs in feedback sessions. A leader might focus heavily on what needs improvement without acknowledging what went well. This imbalance can create the impression that the leader is never satisfied, eroding team members' confidence and motivation.

Finally, leaders can unknowingly alienate team members by subtly showing favoritism. They communicate that some matter more than others by consistently turning to the same person in meetings for opinions or regularly delegating the most desirable projects to a particular subgroup. This might not be deliberate exclusion, but the perception of favoritism can fracture team cohesion and trust.

Leaders must notice how their actions affect others and navigate appropriately to lead effectively. It isn't enough to focus on the work, set high standards, and hold people accountable to those standards. Instead, we must dance around the context within which we operate and navigate through an organization's complex emotional and behavioral landscape. In essence, we need to learn how to find balance in our behaviors and shift those behaviors to meet the situation at hand.

Finding the sweet spot

The story I shared at the beginning of this chapter exemplifies how blind we can be to our actions. Many of us act and react subconsciously and struggle to navigate the complex interplay of expectations, responsibilities, and relationships. We're often influenced by habits, emotions, past experiences, and distracting desires, and these influences cause us to act in unhelpful ways. Essentially, we act in extreme ways and miss the sweet spot of behavior.

The sweet spot is a concept I take from golf, but it is equally applicable when navigating the actions we take in leadership and life. In golf, the sweet spot is a tiny location on the golf club that, when hit, results in the most efficient and effective transfer of energy to the golf ball, sending it far and straight down the fairway. The sweet spot is a tiny part of the golf club, measuring in millimeters, and missing it can have dire consequences. It can be the difference between hitting the golf ball directly at your target or dumping it into a water hazard and incurring a penalty stroke.

When navigating our actions, hitting the sweet spot means finding a precise balance in our behaviors that maximizes positive impact while minimizing negative consequences. This balance is crucial because, like in golf, a miss-hit can lead to outcomes that veer wildly off course, affecting self-esteem, team morale, productivity, and, ultimately, our success.

Hitting the sweet spot requires us to be acutely aware of our behaviors and how others perceive them. It calls for a keen sensitivity to our contexts and the nuances of human relationships. It's about making minute adjustments to ensure our actions are neither harsh nor lenient, rigid nor flexible.

The challenge, of course, is that this sweet spot is not a static target. It shifts and changes depending on the situation, the people involved, and the goals at hand. This means that what works in one context may not work in another, and what succeeds with one team member may fail with another. Understanding this dynamic and being able to adapt accordingly is what sets genuinely effective people apart.

To find the sweet spot more often, we must understand that our actions can manifest in many ways. Here are eight examples that illustrate how subtle shifts in actions can accidentally miss the sweet spot.

ACTION #1: DIRECTING

Directing often stems from the compelling urge to control outcomes and steer projects or people toward a specific end. In leadership, the ability to direct effectively is valuable, but when overemphasized, it can shift from guidance to rigidity.

Have you ever worked with a leader who outlines every project step, leaving no room for team input? The leader's initial intent to ensure project success gradually morphs into a stifling command, quashing creativity and initiative among the team members. In personal relationships, the desire to direct can manifest as micromanagement in family activities or planning, leading to resentment and a lack of spontaneity.

Finding the sweet spot requires us to recognize the value of delegation and trust in others' capabilities. We must let go a little to allow others to contribute, and ideas to flow freely. When a leader operates in the sweet spot, others will see this person as disciplined, decisive, organized, and proactive. Contrast that with someone on overdrive, and people will describe the leader as controlling, overbearing, inflexible, and acting like a micromanager.

ACTION #2: THINKING

Thinking is a critical leadership skill that involves analyzing information and thinking strategically to make well-informed decisions. However, being in overdrive can lead to indecisiveness and a paralyzing level of perfectionism. Consider a leader who constantly weighs every possible outcome and seeks more data before deciding. This approach can stall progress and frustrate team members who are ready to move forward.

In personal situations, overthinking can manifest as never-ending pros and cons lists for simple daily choices. Once someone is stuck in analysis paralysis, it can be challenging to break free. Instead of facilitating a smoother decision-making process, it complicates straightforward situations and delays action, creating stress and inefficiency.

Finding the sweet spot in thinking means balancing thorough analysis with timely decision-making. Leaders who operate in this sweet spot are seen as informed and rational, making decisions based on a reflective and objective assessment of the available information. They know how to gather enough insight to make decisions without falling into the trap of overthinking. This approach allows them to avoid indecisiveness and perfectionism that can hinder a leader's effectiveness and team morale.

ACTION #3: PROTECTING

Protecting ourselves and others from potential harm is a good thing. It's essential for creating a safe working environment but can lead to a cold and detached demeanor when it's taken too far. An overly protective leader might become cynical and see new ideas and change as a potential threat rather than an opportunity. When on overdrive, this behavior can make a leader seem superior, dismissing others' input and isolating themselves from the team they aim to protect.

In personal relationships, protecting manifests as cynicism and withdrawing from others when on overdrive. It stifles growth and keeps people from forming close relationships. Cynicism is often perceived as a sense of superiority that prevents genuine engagement with others. It hinders personal connections and professional collaborations.

Finding the sweet spot in protecting requires us to be prudent and selective. We need to know when to protect and when to allow for calculated risks. Leaders who master this balance are seen as empathetic and understanding of their team's needs and perspectives. They are also seen as resilient and capable of bouncing back from challenges without becoming overly defensive or isolated. This balanced approach ensures that protection doesn't become a barrier to progress but a thoughtful strategy to navigate risks effectively.

ACTION #4: COMPLYING

Complying is an essential act that creates alignment with organizational standards and regulations. It supports harmony and adherence to shared goals within a team. However, when compliance is on overdrive, it can lead to a range of negative behaviors.

Leaders who are too focused on compliance may appear insecure and constantly seek approval before making decisions. This can evolve into passive-aggressive behavior, where they avoid taking the initiative for fear of stepping out of bounds. Over-compliance can also manifest as dependence on higher-ups or established rules, inhibiting innovation and personal judgment. Additionally, excessive compliance can turn into people-pleasing, where decisions are made solely to satisfy others' expectations rather than based on what's best for the team or project.

In personal relationships, this excessive need to comply can prevent individuals from expressing their genuine opinions and needs, leading to dissatisfaction and a lack of authentic relationships. This behavior dampens individuality and erodes trust, as colleagues and friends may perceive the compliant individual as not standing by their values or as someone who cannot lead decisively.

Finding the sweet spot in complying means being cooperative but not overly accommodating. Leaders who strike this balance are considerate and open to the needs and opinions of others without compromising their principles. They are supportive and provide their teams with the guidance needed to adhere to standards while encouraging independent problem-solving. Moreover, they recognize when rules must be upheld and flexibility is required. This balanced approach to complying allows leaders to maintain order and respect without stifling creativity and individual initiative.

ACTION #5: EMPOWERING

Empowering others is a vital aspect of leadership that involves trusting team members with the autonomy to make decisions and act. When done right, it can boost morale and drive innovation. When taken to extremes, empowering can become overwhelming for employees. Leaders may assign too many responsibilities without proper guidance, leading to confusion and stress. This can also manifest as inconsistency, where the leader's expectations are unclear or fluctuate too much, causing team members to feel insecure about their roles and contributions. Additionally, an unfocused approach to empowerment might see leaders demanding too much from their teams without aligning these expectations with clear objectives or providing the necessary resources.

At home, excessive empowerment can burden individuals by imposing unrealistic self-reliance, often without sufficient support or context. Imagine a child with too many responsibilities, such as managing all their school work, extracurricular activities, and household chores, without appropriate guidance. While the intent might be to develop independence, inadequate support and advice can lead to stress, confusion, and feeling overwhelmed, potentially affecting the child's development and self-esteem.

Finding the sweet spot in empowering involves being motivating and inclusive. Leaders who excel in this area inspire their teams by setting clear goals and providing the resources needed to achieve them. They are responsible and ensure that while they delegate tasks, they offer guidance and support, making themselves available to discuss issues and solutions. Additionally, confident leaders trust their decisions to empower others. They create an environment of mutual respect and growth that elevates the team's overall capabilities and builds a strong, collaborative, and committed workforce.

ACTION #6: APPRECIATING

One of the best things we can do is appreciate others for their efforts and achievements. Appreciation creates value and motivation in others and makes us feel good. However, when appreciation is delivered without discernment, it can become inauthentic and condescending. Leaders who constantly praise every action, regardless of its impact or intention, risk diluting the significance of their words, making their commendations seem superficial. Too much appreciation can lead to dependency, where team members no longer feel motivated to excel but perform just enough to gain the leader's approval.

With friends, excessive praise can undermine genuine gratitude and lead others to question the sincerity of your actions. It can create complacency in relationships and stifle the drive for self-improvement. Your words quickly lose meaning if feedback does not accurately reflect people's precise contributions.

Leaders who find the sweet spot in appreciation acknowledge the specific contributions of their team members. They understand that specific recognition reinforces desirable behaviors and enhances team morale, which motivates individuals to continue improving and contributing meaningfully.

ACTION #7: CONNECTING

Connecting is all about building relationships and fostering a collaborative environment. However, it can become counterproductive when leaders overextend their efforts to connect. Leaders who try too hard to forge connections might intrude into personal boundaries, making team members feel uncomfortable rather than supported. This overextension can lead to unfocused interactions that lack a clear purpose, resulting in disorganization rather than meaningful engagement.

In personal contexts, too much emphasis on connecting can overwhelm friends and family, make social interactions feel forced, and leave little room for genuine relationship growth. This overzealous approach can dilute the quality of connections, turning what could be a meaningful interaction into superficial exchange.

Finding the sweet spot for connecting involves being resourceful, supportive, inclusive, and trustworthy. Leaders who excel in this area use their skills to create an environment where everyone feels valued and part of the team. They understand the importance of respecting personal boundaries while making themselves available to support others. This balanced approach strengthens team cohesion and empowers individuals, creating a foundation of trust and mutual respect that enhances collective and individual performance.

ACTION #8: COLLABORATING

Collaboration is incredibly valuable but, taken to extremes, it can also create inefficiencies and adverse outcomes. Leaders who overemphasize collaboration are more likely to avoid conflicts essential for team building. They can also hinder innovation and foster groupthink, which can be counterproductive. In such environments, the desire to maintain harmony and consensus can actually stifle diverse opinions and critical thinking. Too much collaboration can backfire, preventing the team from exploring various solutions and settling too quickly on mediocre ideas.

Excessive collaboration outside of work can complicate simple decisions, as too many opinions are solicited for even the smallest matters. This often hurts relationships, slows things down, and removes personal responsibility from the equation. It frequently leads to frustration among individuals who feel their time and input could be used more effectively elsewhere.

Finding the sweet spot in collaborating involves respecting different viewpoints while pushing for progress. Leaders who do this well make good decisions while including others in the process, but they don't take it to extremes. They encourage respectful dialogue and quickly recognize when to converge on decisions to maintain momentum. This ensures that things get done in a timely fashion while creating the buy-in needed to create sustainable success.

Finding the proper path

Throughout this chapter, we have explored how subtle shifts in actions affect our outcomes. Much like navigating the complexities of a dynamic environment, leadership requires us to find and consistently hit the sweet spot in our behaviors. Whether directing, thinking, protecting, complying, empowering, appreciating, connecting, or collaborating, subtle actions can move us toward success or steer us off course. The challenge lies in maintaining the balance where your actions yield the most positive impact while minimizing unintended consequences.

Participating in a 360° assessment showed me how easy it is to fall into extreme behaviors when driven by a strong desire to achieve. My critical nature often missed the sweet spot and created barriers between me and the team. By embracing nuance and making subtle shifts, I learned to show up in a way that wasn't overly critical or arrogant, and eventually reaped the rewards.

As you move forward, remember that finding the sweet spot is a never-ending process. It requires patience, intention, and a willingness to adjust course when necessary. But by being mindful of the subtle shifts in your actions, you can create a ripple effect that transforms your leadership and has a lasting positive impact on your team and organization. So, the next time you face a challenge, ask yourself: Am I hitting the sweet spot? And if not, what subtle shift can I make to find it?

Leadership
requires us
to find and
consistently hit
the sweet spot.

Chapter Summary

- We succeed or fail because of nuance. The most successful people understand and navigate the fine line between helpful and harmful actions and behaviors.

- Change will only happen if we realize that every moment in our lives is a defining moment, and at every moment, we can choose what we do and how we show up.

- The power of subtle shifts lies in their cumulative effect. Each small change builds on the last, creating a ripple effect that can transform leaders, teams, and organizations.

- Great leaders notice how their actions affect others and adjust appropriately. It isn't enough to focus on the work, set high standards, and hold people accountable to those standards.

- When navigating our actions, hitting the sweet spot means finding a precise balance in our behaviors that maximizes positive impact while minimizing negative consequences.

- There are eight areas where we need to find the sweet spot. They are (1) Directing, (2) Thinking, (3) Protecting, (4) Complying, (5) Empowering, (6) Appreciating, (7) Connecting, and (8) Collaborating.

Conclusion

"The secret of getting ahead is getting started."
~ Mark Twain

In 2008, Lin-Manuel Miranda picked up Ron Chernow's biography of Alexander Hamilton while on vacation. Most people couldn't imagine how an 800-page history book could inspire one of the most successful Broadway musicals ever, but Miranda saw something no one else did. Hamilton's story of ambition, revolution, and reinvention is, in many ways, a modern story. So Miranda envisioned Hamilton as a hip-hop musical, blending the story of America's first treasury secretary with the rhythms of modern rap and R&B. When Miranda announced that he would perform the opening number at the White House in 2009, the audience laughed at the idea. When the performance ended, the audience jumped up for a standing ovation.

It's easy to appreciate the audience's reaction after Hamilton went on to become a huge success but think about how rare it is for us to appreciate what's in front of us when something revolutionary appears. Most of the time, we do the opposite. We dismiss it outright or laugh out of the discomfort it stirs in us. It's not because we're unwilling to change—it's because we don't know how to. We get

Embrace the subtle nature of change.

stuck in the patterns and assumptions we've built over time, and our habits get in our way. But just as the world embraced the innovative nature of Hamilton, I want you to embrace the subtle nature of change. I want you to make subtle shifts in your attention, assumptions, and actions to create significant and sustainable success in your life and the lives of the people you lead.

I started this book by asking you to get off the transformation treadmill. I told you to stop looking for big, bold, dramatic changes because I was sure that your approach was zapping your energy and holding you back. But now I'm confident that you get all that, and I hope you are ready to move forward with a new approach. You've seen how subtle shifts can break old patterns and open the door to something new. You've learned that the key to progress isn't in dramatic overhauls but in the power of consistent, intentional adjustments. Now all you have to do is start making subtle shifts.

The subtle shift roadmap

Here is a road map you can follow to start making subtle shifts immediately. This step-by-step approach is designed to help you implement what you learned in this book, align your focus with what truly matters, and create meaningful progress without feeling overwhelmed.

1. **Clarify your vision.** Reflect on what success looks like for you. Write down your core values, long-term goals, and the impact you want to make. A clear vision will act like a compass, helping you focus on what truly matters.
2. **Identify reactive patterns.** Observe where you feel stuck, reactive, or out of control. Write down specific situations

where you tend to react rather than respond thoughtfully. Awareness of these patterns is the first step to breaking free from them and moving toward more intentional actions.

3. **Audit your attention.** Track how you spend your time and energy for one week. Identify distractions, inefficiencies, or activities that don't align with your priorities. Redirecting your attention to what matters most will lay the foundation for effective shifts.

4. **Challenge your assumptions.** Write down beliefs or assumptions you hold about your capabilities, your environment, or others. Ask yourself, "Is this true? Is there another perspective I haven't considered?" Examining these assumptions will help you uncover new opportunities for growth and creativity.

5. **Focus on small, intentional actions.** Break down big goals into manageable steps. Choose one small, meaningful action to take today that aligns with your vision. These consistent actions will compound over time and create significant results.

6. **Calibrate regularly.** Set aside time weekly to review your attention, assumptions, and actions. Ask, "Am I staying aligned with my vision? What adjustments can I make?" Regular calibration will keep you on track and ensure you're adapting as circumstances evolve.

7. **Engage with feedback.** Seek input from trusted colleagues, mentors, or friends. Ask for honest feedback about how you're showing up and suggestions on how to improve.

External perspectives will help you refine your approach and identify blind spots.

8. **Balance content with context.** Shift your focus from "what needs to be done" (content) to "why it matters and how it fits" (context). For every task, consider how it aligns with the bigger picture. Understanding context will ensure your actions are productive and meaningful.

9. **Embrace creativity over reactivity.** When faced with challenges, pause before reacting. Ask yourself, "What can I create in this situation? How can I move forward with intention?" Shifting to a generative mindset will empower you to shape your circumstances instead of being shaped by them.

10. **Commit to continuous growth.** Invest in lifelong learning through books, courses, mentors, or experiences. Regularly ask yourself, "What else can I learn to help me expand or adjust my assumptions?" A commitment to growth will help you adapt, evolve, and sustain success over time.

Take daily steps to create a deeper sense of clarity, purpose, and adaptability around the shifts you are making. Remember, success isn't about doing everything at once—it's about consistently showing up, recalibrating, and moving forward with intention.

Maintaining your momentum

Momentum is the force that keeps you moving forward when challenges arise or motivation wanes. It isn't built in a single moment and requires intentional effort over time. We must stay committed to subtle shifts to see sustainable results over time. Still, when life throws unexpected challenges your way, return to the three primary shifts at the heart of this book. You'll stay on course by focusing on your attention, assumptions, and actions, no matter what you face.

1. **Shifting attention.** It's easy to get caught up in the noise and distractions of daily life. When that happens, pause and ask yourself, "Am I focused on what matters most right now?" Take a moment to recalibrate—step back, journal, meditate, or talk with a trusted mentor. Revisit your vision and priorities, and use them to guide your next steps.

2. **Shifting assumptions.** When progress feels stalled, it's often because you're operating on autopilot, relying on assumptions that no longer serve you. Challenge those assumptions. Ask, "Is this still true? Is there another way to see this?" Shifting your perspective can unlock creative solutions and uncover opportunities you didn't know existed.

3. **Shifting actions.** Once your attention is clear and your assumptions are reexamined, it's time to take intentional action. Break your goals into small, manageable steps that build momentum and reinforce alignment with your values and vision. Interruptions and competing demands will always try to pull you off track, so use what you've learned

to protect your time, set boundaries, and stay focused on the actions that matter most.

This book has shown that sustainable success is more than dramatic transformations or nonstop hustle. It's about making subtle, incremental shifts that align your life and leadership with what truly matters. These subtle shifts are the key to creating clarity, confidence, and meaningful impact—not just today but for the long haul.

Now is your time. Use what you've learned to make subtle shifts in all areas of life. Start small, start now, and let the journey unfold. Here's to subtle shifts!

Before You Close This Book...

I wrote one chapter that didn't make it into *Subtle Shifts*. Not because it didn't belong, but because it opened a new door. Writing that chapter led to an unexpected insight, which became the seed for my next book. The chapter, called *The Central Shift*, explores how polarized thinking holds us back and how consideration helps us move forward. It's raw, honest, and deeply personal. If this book helped you think differently about change, I think you'll find this bonus chapter just as meaningful.

You can download this chapter at:
mattcross.com/bonus-chapter

About the Author

Matt Cross is an author, speaker, and advisor specializing in leadership and change. Drawing on twenty-five years of experience helping leaders navigate complex challenges, Matt has built a reputation for helping executives, entrepreneurs, and emerging leaders create lasting change with intention and purpose. His insights have supported leadership teams in Fortune 500 companies, pioneering startups, government agencies, and some of the world's leading nonprofits.

Through his popular email newsletter, *The Subtle Shift*, Matt offers practical strategies that empower leaders to approach change with clarity and confidence. Known for his straightforward approach and genuine passion for helping others, Matt is a sought-after speaker, regularly presenting to leaders looking to foster more resilient, cohesive, and high-performing teams.

ABOUT THE AUTHOR

There's nothing Matt values more than making a real difference in people's lives by inspiring them to believe in their potential and take the steps that lead to sustainable success. While his work takes him to many places, Matt stays grounded in the simple joys of family, friendship, and community. He lives in New England with his wife and daughter.

To learn more about Matt, subscribe to his newsletter, or book him for a speaking engagement, visit **https://mattcross.com**

Notes

In this section, you'll find a list of notes, references, and citations for each chapter in *Subtle Shifts*. I tried to accurately attribute the ideas and concepts that have influenced my work, recognizing that much of what we accomplish is, as Isaac Newton so eloquently put it, "standing on the shoulders of giants." The thoughts and insights shared in this book are built upon the wisdom and contributions of those who came before me, and for all of them, I am grateful.

That said, I fully acknowledge the possibility of errors—whether in attributing ideas to the wrong source, overlooking a deserving contributor, or simply misrepresenting a concept. If you believe a mistake has been made, I welcome your input and would appreciate hearing from you. Don't hesitate to contact me at **matt@mattcross.com** so that I can address any inaccuracies and ensure that credit is appropriately given where it is due. I will maintain an up-to-date list of endnotes and corrections at https://mattcross.com/subtleshifts/endnotes.

Preface

1. "Subtle." "Shift." 2011. In: *The American Heritage Dictionary of the English Language*. 5th ed. Boston: Houghton Mifflin Company. https://ahdictionary.com.
2. joshbersin. 2024. "The $340 Billion Corporate Learning Industry Is Poised for Disruption." Josh Bersin. March 23, 2024. https://joshbersin.com/2024/03/the-340-billion-corporate-learning-industry-is-poised-for-disruption/.
3. Wadhwani, Preeti. "Personal Development Market Size - by Instrument (Books, e-Platforms, Personal Coaching/Training, Workshops & Seminars), Focus Area (Mental Health, Motivation & Inspiration, Physical Health, Self-awareness, Skillset Enhancement) & Global Forecast, 2023 - 2032." *Global Market Insights* Inc., September 1, 2023. https://www.gminsights.com/industry-analysis/personal-development-market?gclid=EAIaIQobChMI-OWz44CJiAMVBzcIBR3DwjKiEAAYASAAEgI_U_D_BwE.
4. Reingold, Jennifer. "How to Fail in Business While Really, Really Trying." Fortune, February 22, 2016. https://fortune.com/2014/03/20/how-to-fail-in-business-while-really-really-trying/.
5. Isaacson, Walter. 2011. *Steve Jobs*. Simon & Schuster.
6. Schwantes, Marcel. 2017. "Steve Jobs Once Gave Some Brilliant Management Advice on Hiring Top People. Here It Is in 2 Sentences." Inc.com. October 17, 2017. https://www.inc.com/marcel-schwantes/this-classic-quote-from-steve-jobs-about-hiring-employees-describes-what-great-leadership-looks-like.html.
7. "Shift." 2011. In: *The American Heritage Dictionary of the English Language*. 5th ed. Boston: Houghton Mifflin Company. https://ahdictionary.com.

Introduction

1. Phillips-Caesar, Erica G., Ginger Winston, Janey C. Peterson, Brian Wansink, Carol M. Devine, Balavanketsh Kanna, Walid Michelin, et al. 2015. "Small Changes and Lasting Effects (SCALE) Trial: The Formation of a Weight Loss Behavioral Intervention Using EVOLVE."

Contemporary Clinical Trials 41 (41): 118–28. https://doi.org/10.1016/j.cct.2015.01.003.

2. Rock, David. 2009. "Managing with the Brain in Mind." Strategy+Business. August 27, 2009. https://www.strategy-business.com/article/09306.

3. Kotter, John. 1996. "Leading Change: Why Transformation Efforts Fail." Harvard Business Review. May 1996. https://hbr.org/1995/05/leading-change-why-transformation-efforts-fail-2.

Chapter One

1. Clear, James. 2018. *Atomic Habits: An Easy and Proven Way to Build Good Habits and Break Bad Ones*. Penguin Random House.

2. Pielot, Martin, Karen Church, and Rodrigo de Oliveira. 2014. An In-Situ Study of Mobile Phone Notifications. In: *MobileHCI '14: Proceedings of the 16th International Conference on Human-Computer Interaction with Mobile Devices & Services*. Association for Computing Machinery. pp.233–42.

3. Killingsworth, Matthew A., and Daniel T. Gilbert. "A Wandering Mind Is an Unhappy Mind." Science 330, no. 6006 (2010): 932–32. https://doi.org/10.1126/science.1192439.

4. Griffey, Harriet. 2018. "The Lost Art of Concentration: Being Distracted in a Digital World." The Guardian. October 14, 2018. https://www.theguardian.com/lifeandstyle/2018/oct/14/the-lost-art-of-concentration-being-distracted-in-a-digital-world.

5. Loh, Kep Kee, and Ryota Kanai. 2014. "Higher Media Multi-Tasking Activity Is Associated with Smaller Gray-Matter Density in the Anterior Cingulate Cortex." Edited by Katsumi Watanabe. *PLoS ONE* 9 (9): e106698. https://doi.org/10.1371/journal.pone.0106698.

6. Ophir, Eyal, Clifford Nass, and Anthony D. Wagner. 2009. "Cognitive Control in Media Multitaskers." *Proceedings of the National Academy of Sciences* 106 (37): 15583–87. https://doi.org/10.1073/pnas.0903620106.

7. Burkeman, Oliver. 2022. *Four Thousand Weeks: Time Management for Mortals*. Toronto: Penguin Canada.

8. This idea was inspired by the work of Jack Zenger and Joe Folkman who talk about being an ambidextrous leader. For more, see: Zenger, Jack. 2018. "Results or Relationships: Which Do You Value More? - Thrive Global - Medium.". Thrive Global. May 2, 2018. https://medium.

com/thrive-global/results-or-relationships-which-do-you-value-more-d9c05f2cbccf.

Chapter Two

1. Declan, Liz. 2024. "All 15 Defining Moments in Anakin Skywalker's Fall to the Dark Side." ScreenRant. February 29, 2024. https://screenrant.com/star-wars-anakin-skywalker-dark-side-fall-defining-moments/.
2. Kidder, Rushworth M. 2009. *How Good People Make Tough Choices: Resolving the Dilemmas of Ethical Living.* New York: Harper.
3. Mackay, Jory. 2019. "Screen Time Stats 2018: How Your Phone Impacts Your Workday – RescueTime." RescueTime Blog. April 5, 2019. https://blog.rescuetime.com/screen-time-stats-2018/.
4. Pattison, Kermit. 2008. "Worker, Interrupted: The Cost of Task Switching." Fast Company. Fast Company. July 28, 2008. https://www.fastcompany.com/944128/worker-interrupted-cost-task-switching.
5. Winnick, Michael. n.d. "Putting a Finger on Our Phone Obsession." Dscout.com. https://dscout.com/people-nerds/mobile-touches.
6. This keynote was delivered by the late Doug Silsbee–a fantastic executive coach and wonderful man. He was the founder of presence-based coaching and the author of three books: *The Mindful Coach, Presence-Based Coaching, and Presence-Based Leadership.* For more about Doug's work check out www.presencebasedcoaching.com.
7. Jung, Carl. 2013. *Archetypes and the Collective Unconscious.* Important Books.
8. The concept of the ego as a "craving machine" has been explored by various thinkers. Eckhart Tolle, in his book *A New Earth*, describes the ego as a compulsive, restless force that is never satisfied and constantly seeks external validation, pleasure, and a sense of identity. He argues that the ego is driven by a sense of lack, always wanting more—whether it's power, recognition, material possessions, or even suffering and drama. In Buddhism, the ego is seen as the source of suffering due to its insatiable desires and attachments to impermanent things. In psychology, this concept is also related to the idea of the "hedonic treadmill," where the ego continuously seeks new pleasures but quickly adapts to them, leading to a constant pursuit of new desires without ever achieving lasting contentment.

9. This was inspired by Karen Horney's work on inner conflicts and character structure. Horney, Karen. 1992. *Our Inner Conflicts: A Constructive Theory of Neurosis*. New York: Norton.

Chapter Three

1. Conscious Leadership is discussed by many, but I want to thank Jim Dethmer from The Conscious Leadership Group for introducing me to this concept. Dethmer, Jim, Diana Chapman, and Kaley Klemp. 2015. *The 15 Commitments of Conscious Leadership: A New Paradigm for Sustainable Success*. United States: Conscious Leadership Group.
2. Sun Tzu. 2017. *The Art of War*. Lexington, Ky: Filiquarian Publishing.
3. Gettysburg Pennsylvania. 2016. "Battle History | Gettysburg PA." Gettysburgpa.gov. https://www.gettysburgpa.gov/history/slideshows/battle-history.
4. Katie Bo Lillis, Jim Sciutto, Kristin Fisher and Natasha Bertrand. 2024. "Exclusive: Russia Attempting to Develop Nuclear Space Weapon to Destroy Satellites with Massive Energy Wave, Sources Familiar with Intel Say | CNN Politics." CNN. February 17, 2024. https://www.cnn.com/2024/02/16/politics/russia-nuclear-space-weapon-intelligence/index.html.
5. Deyan, Georgiev. 2024. "17 Eye-Opening Zoom Statistics to Show How Big It Is in 2023." Techjury. September 25, 2024. https://techjury.net/blog/zoom-statistics/.
6. Banyai, Istvan. 2012. *Zoom*. London: Puffin.
7. McCormick, Patricia. 1995. "All Things Reconsidered." The New York Times . November 12, 1995. https://www.nytimes.com/1995/11/12/books/all-things-reconsidered.html.
8. "Zoom by Istvan Banyai, Astvan Banyai." 2024. Publishersweekly.com. https://www.publishersweekly.com/9780670858040.

Chapter Four

1. Geiger, Soren. 2019. "Churchill's Character: A Rigid Daily Schedule." The Churchill Project - Hillsdale College. February 6, 2019. https://winstonchurchill.hillsdale.edu/churchill-character-daily-schedule/.

2. Newport, Cal. 2016. *Deep Work: Rules for Focused Success in a Distracted World*. London: Piatkus.
3. Holiday, Ryan. 2019. *Stillness Is the Key: An Ancient Strategy for Modern Life*. London: Portfolio/Penguin, An Imprint Of Penguin Random House Llc.
4. Adler, Mortimer Jerome, and Charles Lincoln Van Doren. 1972. *How to Read a Book*. Revised and Updated edition, Touchstone published by Simon & Schuster.
5. Georghiades, Petros. 2004. "From the General to the Situated: Three Decades of Metacognition." *International Journal of Science Education* 26 (3): 365–83. https://doi.org/10.1080/0950069032000119401.
6. Farnsworth, W. 2021. *The Socratic method: a practitioner's handbook*. Boston: Godine.
7. Gallup. 2024. "CliftonStrengths." Gallup.com. https://www.gallup.com/cliftonstrengths/en/252137/home.aspx.
8. James P. Gray. 2013. "It's a Gray Area: Einstein's Brilliant Thoughts Pertinent to Today's Woes." Daily Pilot. The Los Angeles Times. May 31, 2013. https://www.latimes.com/socal/daily-pilot/opinion/tn-dpt-me-0602-gray-20130531-story.html.
9. The idea that information is abundant is fascinating to me. The amount of data created every day is staggering and continues to grow rapidly. As of 2024, it is estimated that approximately 328.77 million terabytes of data are generated daily. For more see GilPress. 2024. "How Much Data Is Generated Every Day (2024)." What's the Big Data? May 9, 2024. https://whatsthebigdata.com/data-generated-every-day/.

Chapter Five

1. Pandey, Prateekshit, Yoona Kang, Nicole Cooper, Matthew O'Donnell, and Emily B Falk. 2021. "Social Networks and Neural Receptivity to Persuasive Health Messages." *Health Psychology* 40 (4): 285–94. https://doi.org/10.1037/hea0001059.
2. Various sources outline how cults work but I found this the most entertaining. "How to Become a Cult Leader." 2023. Documentary. Netflix.

3. Nelson, Portia. 2012. *There's a Hole in My Sidewalk*. London: Simon & Schuster.

Chapter Six

1. Copernicus, Nicolaus. (1543) 1995. *On the Revolutions of the Heavenly Spheres*. Amherst: Prometheus Books.
2. The quote "No army can stop an idea whose time has come" is commonly attributed to Victor Hugo. However, it appears that the exact wording of this popular quote does not directly appear in Hugo's works. Instead, it is likely a paraphrased or evolved version of a sentiment expressed by Hugo in his book *Histoire d'un crime* (The History of a Crime), published in 1877. In this work, Hugo wrote: "On résiste à l'invasion des armées; on ne résiste pas à l'invasion des idées," which translates to "One resists the invasion of armies; one does not resist the invasion of ideas". For more see: "Quote Origin: Nothing Is More Powerful than an Idea Whose Time Has Come – Quote Investigator®." 2023. Quoteinvestigator.com. November 6, 2023. https://quoteinvestigator.com/2023/11/05/powerful-idea/.

Chapter Seven

1. Carpenter, C. C. J., Joseph A. Durick, Rabbi Hilton J. Grafman, Bishop Paul Hardin, Bishop Holan B. Harmon, George M. Murray, Edward V. Ramage, and Earl Stallings. "A Call for Unity." *Birmingham News*, April 13, 1963.
2. King, Martin Luther. 2011. *Why We Can't Wait*. Boston: Beacon Press.
3. Porter, Michael. 1996. "What Is Strategy?" Harvard Business Review. 1996. https://hbr.org/1996/11/what-is-strategy.
4. Lafley, A G, and Roger L Martin. 2013. *Playing to Win: How Strategy Really Works*. Boston (Ma): Harvard Business Review Press.
5. Mikael Cho, "Steve Jobs Saved Apple—and Nike—with the Same Piece of Advice," Quartz, January 18, 2017. https://qz.com/884489/steve-jobs-saved-apple-and-nike-with-the-same-piece-of-advice.

Chapter Eight

1. Kahneman, Daniel and Amos Tversky. "Intuitive Prediction: Biases and Corrective Procedures," *Decision Research Technical Report* PTR-1042-77-6 1977. https://apps.dtic.mil/sti/pdfs/ADA047747.pdf.

2. The quote "In preparing for battle I have always found that plans are useless, but planning is indispensable" is commonly attributed to Dwight D. Eisenhower, but the exact origin of this quote is somewhat unclear. For more "Plans Are Worthless, but Planning Is Everything – Quote Investigator." 2017. Quoteinvestigator.com. November 18, 2017. https://quoteinvestigator.com/2017/11/18/planning/.

3. Mike Berardino. 2012. "Mike Tyson Explains One of His Most Famous Quotes." South Florida Sun Sentinel. November 9, 2012. https://www.sun-sentinel.com/2012/11/09/mike-tyson-explains-one-of-his-most-famous-quotes-3/.

4. Vikas Mittal, Alessandro Piazza, and Ashwin Malshe. May 1, 2023. "Is Your Company as Strategically Aligned as You Think It Is?," Harvard Business Review. https://hbr.org/2023/05/is-your-company-as-strategically-aligned-as-you-think-it-is?.

5. Efron, Louise. 2022. "Are Your Company Values More than Just Words?" Gallup.com. December 14, 2022. https://www.gallup.com/workplace/406418/company-values-words.aspx.

6. Efron, Louise. 2022. "Are Your Company Values More than Just Words?" Gallup.com. December 14, 2022. https://www.gallup.com/workplace/406418/company-values-words.aspx.

7. Sull, Donald, Stefano Turconi, Charles Sull, and James Yoder. 2017. "Turning Strategy into Results." MIT Sloan Management Review. September 28, 2017. https://sloanreview.mit.edu/article/turning-strategy-into-results/.

Beyond the Book

Explore the Services Behind Subtle Shifts

If you need help applying what you learned in this book, Matt offers a range of services to support leaders, teams and organizations:

Keynotes & Interactive Workshops
Matt regularly brings the ideas behind Subtle Shifts to life through high-energy, story-driven keynotes and highly interactive workshops. These experiences help leaders translate subtle ideas into real-world action. Most requested sessions include:

- The Profound Power of Subtle Shifts
- Subtle Shifts for Teams
- Subtle Shifts for Leaders
- Subtle Shifts in Communication

Executive Coaching
Matt's coaching engagements are built on the belief that meaningful change starts from within. Drawing from the Subtle Shifts framework, Matt helps leaders uncover blind spots, recalibrate behaviors, and lead with more presence, clarity, and intention. His approach is

trusted by executives, founders, and emerging leaders who are ready to grow, not just in their roles, but as people.

Subtle Shifts Group Coaching

This small-group coaching experience combines the insight of executive coaching with the power of peer-to-peer learning. Designed for high-potential leaders and mid-level managers, Subtle Shifts Group Coaching provides a safe, structured environment for exploring mindset, leadership habits, and personal growth alongside others on a similar journey.

The Subtle Shift Newsletter

Each week, Matt shares one small but powerful idea to help you lead with clarity, inspire change, and create a lasting impact. It's free, practical, and designed to help you stay grounded in what matters most.

Learn more at mattcross.com

www.ingramcontent.com/pod-product-compliance
Lightning Source LLC
LaVergne TN
LVHW041916070526
838199LV00051BA/2634